BROKEN FOR GOOD

BROKEN FOR GOOD

HOW GRIEF AWOKE
MY GREATEST HOPES

———— ✦ ————

REBECCA RENE JONES

New York   Boston   Nashville

Unless otherwise indicated, all Scripture quotations are taken from the *Holy Bible: New International Version* (NIV). Copyright © 1973, 1978, 1984, 2011 by Biblica, Inc. Used by permission of Zondervan. All rights reserved worldwide. (www.zondervan.com)

Scriptures noted NLT are from the *Holy Bible*, New Living Translation, copyright © 1996. Used by permission of Tyndale House Publishers, Inc., Wheaton, Illinois 60189. All rights reserved.

Scriptures noted KJV are taken from the King James Version of the Holy Bible.

FaithWords
Hachette Book Group
1290 Avenue of the Americas
New York, NY 10104
www.faithwords.com

Printed in the United States of America

RRD-C

First Edition: April 2016

10 9 8 7 6 5 4 3 2 1

FaithWords is a division of Hachette Book Group, Inc.
The FaithWords name and logo are trademarks of Hachette Book Group, Inc.

The Hachette Speakers Bureau provides a wide range of authors for speaking events. To find out more, go to www.hachettespeakersbureau.com or call (866) 376-6591.

The publisher is not responsible for websites (or their content) that are not owned by the publisher.

Library of Congress Cataloging-in-Publication Data has been applied for.

ISBN 978-1-4555-3806-5

This one's for you, Dad.

Every man's life is a fairy-tale written by God's fingers.
—Hans Christian Andersen, "The Finger of God"

CONTENTS

Author's Note   xi

Chapter One: No Round-Trip Flights   1

Chapter Two: The Man Who Drank a Lake   4

Chapter Three: Lots of Knocking   16

Chapter Four: Ties as Tissues   32

Chapter Five: Holy Mud   49

Chapter Six: Sorting Laundry   60

Chapter Seven: Newton for Newton   82

Chapter Eight: A Rose for a Thorn   92

Chapter Nine: One More Jump   111

Chapter Ten: Lawnmower Man   128

Chapter Eleven: All You Can Eat   146

Chapter Twelve: A Highway   156

Chapter Thirteen: The Long Way Home   170

Chapter Fourteen: Tucking in Tight   177

Chapter Fifteen: Forget the Harps   190

Commission: The Best Kind of Hungry   197

Acknowledgments   203

Notes   205

AUTHOR'S NOTE

On Names and Other Small Details

Memory is a fickle friend, but for all her faults, there's no denying: She's also wonderfully protective. Our minds, mercifully, sometimes scrub the truly dangerous. We *unremember*. We edit, elide, so we can exist.

This can make memoir-craft slippery business, especially when you're reaching across the space of ten years, trying to resurrect poignant moments in stunning retinal display. This is my best attempt to tell a story—my story, of loving my father, and losing my father, and finding him all over again. Written in fits and spasms over the course of a decade, some parts are still white-hot, the wounds of raw, bubbling grief; others were penned while but faintly bruised; still more as my fingers softly swept over scars, reverent, slowly starting to hope again. Grief is a messy process. Writing about it is messier. I would not wish it on anyone.

That said, please know that I have strived to be as honest as possible in my restoration; it's no small thing to steward such sacred truths. I want to be fair to my family, and especially, to my father.

In the pages that follow, I've changed some names—sometimes at the individual's request, sometimes on my own good hunch.

And since my mind is Teflon to niggling details—and fresh story-telling demands them—I've taken some small liberties when the writer in me said it absolutely mattered, when I was certain these soft brushstrokes wouldn't compromise the bigger story.

Thank you, in advance, for the grace.

BROKEN FOR GOOD

Chapter One

NO ROUND-TRIP FLIGHTS

Everyone can master a grief but he that has it.
—William Shakespeare, *Much Ado About Nothing*

God arranges a world in six days.

Straining night from day, and pooling oceans, he stocks them with prawns and plankton, coral kingdoms. Swordfish, sea urchins, sharks, and stingrays. Dolphins. The double-blowhole humpback whale.

He plants redwoods, evergreens, hangs high the North Star. Fastens tissuey wings on buzzing green beetles, then whiskers on kittens. Slowly, he stretches brontosauri necks strong, long, like he's rolling soft pretzels. They're Play-Doh in his palms.

Scattering sunflowers by the fieldful, he smooths a carpet of seaweed. Then there's clover and cacti and coconut trees, petunias and pussy willows and poinsettias. The darting dance of pollination, black-and-yellow drones weaving a world together. Ears of corn shoot skyward, potatoes burrow below, as bunches of grapes erupt from the vine, spilling royal skins taut, tart, hot in the afternoon sun.

The party is just getting started.

Enter horses, hippos, hermit crabs. Cue the foxes, flamingos, finches, flying frogs.

Behold the feathers of the macaw, a head-to-toe rainbow, colored with every Crayola in the box. See the plumage of peacocks, the turkey's wiggly wattle, blubbery penguins braving the cold, not a shiver. Mix in migratory patterns, mating calls, that fierce mothering instinct. Cocoon naps, moon-pull tides, silk-spinning worms, fall's fiery leaves. And still, we're water striders, only skimming the surface.

Go deeper, and find atoms, acoustics, acceleration—intrinsic forces and immutable laws that help all hang together. Energy, equilibrium. Reflection, refraction.

Genetics. Gravity.

Grace.

This, a boundless banquet of beauty, a peek into the playground of the infinite mind. It is so good. Over and over, that's the refrain: God nods, and *it is good*.

But is it enough?

To crown it all, God breathes life into dust, and they rise, two jewels: man, woman, and a magnetic, mysterious love that pulls flesh to flesh, two into one.

You take that idea, and you extrapolate it. It's simple math, really—almost painfully so. If this creation—so shaken down, pressed into our laps, overflowing—is the handiwork of a six-day God, shouldn't it follow that heaven, the paradise Jesus says he's been fussing with for, oh, just *thousands* of years, is going to have better amenities? The most coveted coffee, in-room Wi-Fi, whatever it is that wins five-star status? Between the 14-carat streets, crystalline seas, thundering throne, and pearly gates (maybe metaphors, maybe not), I bet it makes Disney World look like a backyard swing set. The kind that hiccups a little when you pump your legs too hard, too high.

See, I never doubted that heaven is trump. *Move over, earth: You've medaled silver. You're the fast-forgotten runner-up. Heaven wins!*

I believe these headlines, always have. In fact, my hope, my Christian faith, is tied up in *precisely* this. Which is why I can't fathom why, when my dad died of melanoma, everyone assumed I'd somehow forgotten. Maybe I'd contracted a case of grief-amnesia.

It was the first thing they'd remind me of.

"But Becky, remember, he's in a far *better* place. Try and *cling* to that."

They didn't know that, as I nodded, I wanted to muzzle them. I put on a dutiful smile, soft-biting my tongue, but inside—oh, how I ached. My hands itched for needle and thread, anything to stitch their lips together, to block further assault. How could I tell them that this—their make-it-better mojo, their *cling-to-this* hope—was just another fancy way of rephrasing the problem? That my dear dad was in an enviable, painless place, yes, but it was immeasurably far away—another dimension, even, and I couldn't exactly pop in for a visit?

This is not a quibble about the accommodations, but the distance.

Because I was *here*.

Dad was *there*.

My arms are too short to reach up, grab his ankles, yank him down.

Go ahead, I dared. Fix *that*.

Chapter Two

THE MAN WHO DRANK A LAKE

All the days ordained for me were written in your book before one of them came to be.

—Psalm 139:16b

Since I was fifteen, my mother has kept a summer cottage on a lake so small that there's actually a rule capping the number of water-skiers to three at a time—and wait, it gets worse: They must be going clockwise.

I kid not.

But the cottage's quirks are the cottage's charm, and they've made us fall in love with it. Just an hour south of Rochester, our lake (or pond, depending on which map's talking) is tucked into New York's Finger Lakes region, just south of relative giants like Canandaigua, Keuka. It's a quick drive from a handful of enterprising young wineries, potato farms, antique shops—all navigable by rambling, hope-your-brakes-work roads.

Our little lakelet, hidden in the hills, bubbles up from nowhere. It's fed by a fretwork of cold springs—icy, underwater geysers that sneak up on you as you swim—and we love this. We love how the lake's a ready-or-not game of hide-and-seek, liquid land mines just waiting to find your toes.

We love that you can be anywhere on the lake, tiny as it is, and still hear Mom call you in for dinner. We love yelping when we jump in and our toes brush the mud-pudding bottom. And secretly, I think we might even love the looming threat of meeting a beefy, brown dock spider—the kind that sleep by the swim ladder and, if rumor's true, can hold their breath for a half hour while they hunt minnows.

"Sparkle time" comes a bit before supper, when the sun slinks below the tree line, skipping rays like rocks across water. This last wedge of lemony light barrels in, unapologetic, through a row of dusty windows, and the lake is electric, a blue–white disco ball, spastic, sending glittering orbs to dance on the cottage ceiling. Someone sees them and runs to ring the old ship's bell that's hung on the wall, and we all look up and grin, taking them in, these small fairies flickering. They will last maybe a minute or two, so we stop, luxuriate, laugh at these silly summertime rituals; secretly, we're just a little bit low that another day has lazed by. How?

This is about the hour Mom inserts her Benny Goodman Orchestra CD (as teens, we groaned) and smushes the player's speakers right up to the tatty window screen, subjecting the whole little lake to her happy, jittering jazz. Dad saunters over to light the grill, then ducks back into the kitchen to make sure the lime marinade has worked its magic. This is probably the best time to unleash the paddleboat and try to hook a pickerel (ostensibly escaping the big band, which, like the dock spiders, we probably secretly like).

The septic acts up when you put showers back-to-back (with three sisters, that's inevitable), and we turn up our noses, aghast, and ask *For heaven's sake, what's that smell?* Like we do not know. And that's Mom's signal; she recites her favorite sermon, all fire and brimstone as she denounces the sin of stacked showers. Every time. We parishioners look up from our books to repent, to beg forgiveness, but plan to promptly forget tomorrow, in the name of smooth-shaven legs.

The whole place leans south, and half the cupboards squeak; the others won't close. The cottage is molting red paint on its backside, and every summer we lift a mug of iced tea, boldly vowing to sand, to prime, repaint. The next spring, it's still shedding, and the dock has sprung a warped plank; it needs a new nail, a good beating back down.

Perfectly imperfect, that's how we love it.

It's the lake.

Growing up, a trip to the lake was synonymous with sun worship. Nights huddled around a fire, mouths flooded with molten marshmallow. It was a free pass from our turn at mowing the lawn, our nightly after-dinner dish duty.

Oh the joy of paper plates, plastic forks.

There were marathon Monopoly games on drizzly days, while Mom pouted from the couch, thumbing through *Woman's Day* and quietly cursing clouds. We feasted at breakfast, plates piled with Belgian waffles, cantaloupe, heaps of home fries reincarnated from last night's salt potatoes.

Rochester is a place poor in sun, but the lake is our Canaan, our paradise flowing. Somewhere along the way, over the years, the lake became summer. And summer became the lake.

And now, the two are so wonderfully muddled, they are downright indissoluble: Give me a scalpel, and I still can't work them apart.

As an adult, now, I cherish the lake for other reasons. Chief among them: Somehow, the lake is the one place where Dad still lives, even all these years later. It's the one place he hasn't been swept up, organized, inadvertently put away.

Really—we feel him here. When someone loves a place so much, they imprint on it; they own it in ways that transcend property rights, even their own heartbeat. Something about the lake *is* Dad. It always will be.

Open the door to the back room, hear the squeak of the hinge: This fishing closet is still arranged (or, unarranged) more or less his way. A musty mess. Eight or more poles, rigged with jigs, stand at sharp attention, ready to cast. There's the tan tackle box, an old minnow pail, a tangle of nets, orange anchors, armfuls of scratchy plastic rope. The mayhem reigns.

His favorite coffee mug—the one whose handle is a small-mouth bass, curved into a leaping *C*—sits in an upper cupboard, to the left of the sink, awaiting an old yellow carafe of early-morning joe.

His rowboat, dubbed *Dishwasher* (inherited from *his* dad, my grandpa John, who bought it with the funds Grandma had earmarked for an appliance), bobs patiently, eager for the next adventure.

One of his proudest photographs hangs on the wall—a perfectly pedestrian sunset he snapped over Lake George, and he'd made sure to byline it, a paper plaque with his name taped inside the glass of the frame. His rock CDs lean against the boom box, his hair pick's in a dresser drawer, and, if you rummage around, you might even find one of those twenty-five-cent pocket note-books housing his chicken-scratch to-do list.

It's funny that this is the place Dad's memory lives, because for me, it's the place he began to die.

It's Independence Day morning, 2001, and the cottage reeks of breakfast, like it took a bath in syrup.

It is already hot, but Mom is coolly arranging pick-'n'-mix candies, the cheap, hard tiny barrels no one really eats, wrapped in patriotic blue-and-red foil, placing them in glass dishes around the cottage. A big supper is planned—fried chicken and those rolls you can peel into a hundred fine skins, the kind that explode from the tube like firecrackers. I am seventeen, appropriately terrified of saturated fat and carbs, which make tonight's buttered potatoes public enemy number one. That, and the strawberry shortcake. I'm full just thinking of it.

It's hot.

My sisters and I are planning to work up an appetite the only way we know how: spending the afternoon swimming, sun-ning on the dock, sipping pink Crystal Light, and whacking one another with foam float noodles.

It's a veritable oven in the bedroom upstairs, and the speckled linoleum is sticky under our feet as we slip into swimsuits, leaving the straps to dangle around our necks so we can help rub sunscreen on each other's shoulders. I'm a kind of kindling; I burn and crin-kle quick, like newsprint. And I hate putting on sunscreen.

Then the knock.

"Girls?"

It's Mom, knocking on the wall beside the doorway—because the door's not really a door. It's a faded orange curtain.

"We're decent," yells Rachel, the oldest (and loudest).

Mom pulls back the curtain, ducking through, like she's coming onstage, eyes tentative. She gathers her hands, almost praying, like she needs something, someone, to hold on to.

"Your dad's been a bit grumpy this weekend," she says.

It's the understatement of the century. Dad's been downright prickly; yesterday, he barked at a grocery clerk who dared to offer a choice between paper and plastic. The boy was my age.

Paper! he'd roared, and the boney boy had looked down to his shoes, fingers moving quick. I'd wanted to crawl beneath the candy rack.

I look up at Mom now, hold this breath. Mom and Dad don't justify each other's behavior. People are what they *do*. Actions are supposed to stand up on their own.

"I'm not excusing him, but there's a lot on his mind."

I brace for what's next, but I already know. It's the way her mascara's smudged a bit in the corners. It's the fact that Mom has come up into our room, now, and that her cheeks are hanging just a little too loose, the way Coach says you're supposed to let them flap and fly free when you run, so you can put all your best energy down into your feet. That's it: that Mom is putting all her energy into saying something, well, that itself says everything.

Remission is over.

"The melanoma's back," she says, like I've got some teleprompter on my forehead, as she mouths my worst thoughts, turns fear into cold, hard fact. "And it's spread."

No one says anything, but a slight gust tickles the curtains then; they billow, lace hems lift and fall leisurely, like gossamer seeds. I pull a beach towel tight around my shoulders. My back's still buttery, wet.

Danielle, two years my junior, bites a lip.

"Does this mean...?" she ventures, and the question hangs. I remember how the sun came in, at that moment—how the hot morning wind kept licking the curtains. Again, *huff*, up. The swell, the float, the soft, fine fall. Like the cottage itself was breathing, hard and slow, taking this in right with us.

Mom nods, no way around. "When cancer comes back, it's never good."

The breeze keeps caressing the cotton, but the small bedroom feels stiff and stale. Our throats stop up.

No one moves.

No one speaks.

Yet our minds are somersaulting. We stand there, sunscreen-slick and statue-still, struggling to swallow this impossible joke in one big bite.

Mom told me, later, that she'd found out that same day, about an hour earlier. Dad had asked her to take a walk around the lake, and right at the point where the road reaches a soft rise, a hill where the little gray pebbles end and the path frays at the wood's edge, he'd dead-stopped walking. The doctor had told him.

And there, with the best bit of the lake in full view, he'd told her.

You would think news like that would spoil a weekend, but you'd be wrong.

We all left the bedroom debriefing intent on soldiering on, being strong.

Which was surprisingly easy; we were numb.

We still swam. We overate, we sunburned. We watched other cottagers' fireworks—smuggled up over the Pennsylvania border—and laughed as neighbors dueled, missile for missile, a booming bouquet dissolving into our stretch of sky. Such showmanship for this must-ski-clockwise lake.

Bottle rockets; fizzing sparklers, waving the wands, writing cursive in the sky; a bright red flare blinking on the end of the dock. We did it all, ducking back into yesterday's oblivion—or trying to. We clung to our last little bit of normal. Cancer was still an idea in our heads then; a word, maybe, but not a monster to wrestle. We could tuck it away. Dad was so good at pretending, and we gratefully played right along.

The thing is, it didn't stop that night. That's how it would be. That's how Dad would die. His cancer didn't slow us down, not for a long time. He adopted a let's-ignore-it policy, and we weren't supposed to discuss it. Not even the three nights a week, before bed, when I gave him his interferon—an investigative, injectable drug. The medicine's natural, a kind of warning protein; it contains a bunch of little Paul Reveres, horseback criers, that ride all night and rouse the body, telling it to boot up for fight. At seventeen, I played nurse, pinching a fold of his thigh, or his upper arm, driving the needle down, administering five clicks of that pen syringe—I always counted slow, careful with this small vial of hope, being sure to squeeze not four, but the full five; making sure every last little click and life-drop and tiny protein was planted good and deep. Re-snapping the cap on the vial, I'd gently dab that one perfect bead of blood, and Dad would cock his head, clinical, complimenting my needle-sticking skills.

"Not too painful today," he'd say, matter-of-fact as a weatherman. "Just a pinch, really."

Those few minutes a night were the only moments that we, together, ever openly acknowledged that he was sick. And even then, we sort of danced around it, a do-si-do; it was happening, but it was not. It was more of a nighttime ritual now, routine as toothbrushing.

Life slowed for Dad, but at a rate we barely noticed. He was so proud, so convinced he could stem the tide. He kept teaching students at the Catholic high school my cousins attended, and I helped him keep dyeing his hair, once a month in the kitchen sink. Just for Men, darkest brown, smelled like lemon and vomit—and looked like I was shampooing him in chocolate syrup. But I kept painting him, big blobs of it all over his temples, where the cancer had salted him white. Eight minutes later, he'd rinse and towel off, inspect my work in the mirror. And finding the patches gone, he'd exclaim, *"I'm new!"* Then he'd pull on a clean sweater and pack up his speakers in the back of the van, one more Saturday night gig with his forty-year-old-guys' group, Rock Bottom.

It wasn't until he quit eating dinner with us that we knew, though no one spoke it. Dad took to a yogurt-only diet and his doctor told us we could stop the shots. For months after he died, those unused boxes of interferon would sit in our refrigerator. Thousands of dollars' worth of medicine, keeping company with dill pickles.

The August after Mom first tells us, in the bedroom—only thirteen months from the Independence Day he began to die—we all drive down for Dad's final trip to the lake. No one calls it that, of course. But we know it.

It's after dinner, the patio table cleared, de-crumbed, mustard and ketchup stowed back in the fridge, and I am on the upper deck, right off the kitchen, riffling through an old magazine when Mom asks me for the favor.

"Could you carry the circular saw up from the dock, and put it back in the tool closet?"

I smile and nod, setting *Seventeen* down. I am the pole-vaulter; I can do more pull-ups than almost any other girl in school. If Mom appeals to my vanity, I'll do just about anything.

I start picking my way down stone steps—they wobble, they're loose—and my walk turns into a little jog, and I start stretching my arms for the feat. The lift. But just before I'm all the way down, I pause.

At the end of the dock, Dad sits in a red aluminum rocker. It's a chair he sanded and spray-painted just two summers earlier. Alone, his back to me, he takes a pull of green tea and swallows slow. He rests the glass on his thigh—or his thighbone—and it is quiet enough that I hear the ice cubes clink.

He sits there, barely stirring, watching this late-summer scene unfold, taking it in.

I take it in, too.

There's the fatty hiss of hot dogs, sputtering as skins split on a neighbor's grill.

Forgotten Dixie cups of lemonade litter our dock, half-full, sun-warmed and sour.

Young boys hoot, holler, taunt, waging a splashy battle on an old tire inner tube just a couple of cottages down the east shore. The fight is fierce, and the opponents well matched. There's lots of good screaming. And laughing.

Then the blip of a fish rustles the glass top of the water, exciting a ring that grows bigger, bigger, bigger, so big it is gone.

I feel the salty film of dried sweat, a second skin on my forehead. A flag hangs, lazy and limp, on our post at the end of the dock. All around this ring of lake, the cottage people crawl, slow, with nowhere, really, that they need to go. And we watch.

Summer.

I squint as the sun sets across the lake and a perfect afternoon melts away. Dad doesn't sip again for some time. He doesn't even really like the taste of tea, he's said—it just soothes his stomach. It's quick sugar. Even yogurt has lost its appeal, lately.

I watch Dad as he's watching everything, and that's when the realization pierces, slices me, really, stabbing so hard and swift that I know I will carry it always, forever. *This moment is sacred*, I think. *I am here, witnessing something herculean.* My father attempting a task that's bigger than he is.

Far bigger.

To everyone else this August afternoon, he is just a man, chair dragged right up to the edge of a dock, drinking a cup of cold tea.

But I know. I know the truth.

Here is a man trying to do something more, something impossible.

Here, in front of me, is a man trying to drink in a lake.

I don't want to ruin this moment. There is something beautiful in Dad, something I'd pay to see in myself. It's a keen approval of the richness, the dimensionality, the wild beauty of a world he is soon leaving. I stand behind, in the long stretch of his shadow, watching him love our little lake as much as he can, trying to memorize each detail, sop up each sunray, sponging the splendor, summer spilled all around.

It's time. Just before he can catch me watching, I squat down and take a deeply dramatic breath, announcing my presence, true, but also rallying strength as I prepare to hoist the saw, to lift what Dad cannot.

But the saw comes up easily, and I gasp.

The saw is light, too light—much lighter than I'd expected.

Dad turns to say thanks, but I am already hurrying back up the stairs, willing all my waters to stay tucked in, telling myself not to cry.

Dad clung on for two more weeks, and then, on a Wednesday at three in the morning—on St. Mary's hospice floor with me, my mom, and my sisters at his side—he quit trying to absorb it all, and he let go.

Chapter Three

LOTS OF KNOCKING

Rivers know this: there is no hurry. We shall get there some day.
—A. A. Milne, *Pooh's Little Instruction Book*

Three years back.

It's 9 a.m. on a Saturday and we're assembled at the kitchen table. Yawning. Dad is at the head, a mug of coffee by his left hand and a brown paper lunch sack pulled over his right. It's a puppet: He's doodled happy eyes and a big pointy nose, and a rotini curl of hair on top. And there's a name tag: BOBBY.

Rachel rolls her eyes; she's still in her pink leopard pajamas. "*What* is going on?"

Dad gives us a fake smile that's all teeth, like he's proving he's flossed; that's our cue.

Sigh.

Family meeting.

But Dad doesn't talk: Bobby does. A pitchy little helium voice that's too enthusiastic for first-thing Saturday.

"Ladies and...ladies...I'm your spokes...bag. Bobby. Yes: I'm Bobby the Bag."

Oh my.

"Dad."

He doesn't break act. Stays chipper. "I'm not Dad, I'm Bobby. And you're probably wondering why we're all gathered here."

We groan. Wondering? More like dreading.

"I'm here to announce the kickoff of an exciting new campaign: O—T—B."

He pauses—and Bobby cranes his neck-body around the circle to gauge reactions.

"Anyone know what OTB stands for?"

Don't ask, don't ask, don't ask.

"Okay, okay, I'll spare you the suspense: OTB is On The Ball."

And then, he winds up and blows his voice out big, like a bullhorn. Says it again in singsong-shout: "ON THE BALL, folks. This weekend: The Sillick family's going to get *ON THE BALL!*"

And then Bobby gets right to basics, breaks it down, and OTB crystallizes, comes into horrible focus. Sure it sounds fun and pithy and progressive, but we aren't fooled: This is classic Dad, window-dressing a whole lot of work. OTB is Saturday's death sentence, because OTB means we are going to rake the backyard.

And stack firewood.

And then, if we really want to get wild: maybe even slice through the jungle that is the basement toy room turned teen club room turned can't-open-the-door-anymore junk room.

Minus the extravagance of a lunch sack emceeing our kitchen table conferences, we are an average American family. We are firm about sitting down to dinner, mostly a lot of lackluster permutations of noodle casserole and shake-in-the-bag chicken and macaroni mixed with frozen peas; we tussle over riding shotgun, and who rode last time; we get irked when someone borrows a sweater from our closet without asking.

We are wonderfully typical. And so, when Dad gets sick, and Bobby dies, we live out the standard cancer story, the one that usually ends the same way.

But stories have a trouble to them, a way of snowballing and packing on weight and growing bigger as we repeat them. And in this one, I must be careful to not glorify my father.

He was an ordinary guy. A computer teacher, which now seems as silly as saying a sleeping teacher, or an eating teacher, but this was back when kids weren't born knowing how to do the iPad finger-swipe.

He was not quite six feet, a good boxy build, and smelled like all fathers should: sunkissed, with a faint hint of sweat and earth, like a garden tomato. And he was frugal, and incurably frumpy, and he liked to flaunt it, announcing that his loafers smelled like Limburger cheese, and once wearing a pair of reversible cotton shorts for nearly a week straight, flipping them back and forth: the blue side, then the maroon. He preferred a pair of blue Saucony sneakers so beat up that his big toe stuck out, and all his jeans went velvety in the knees long before he took out Mom's kitchen shears and sliced them down to shorts.

He was a forager, too. He bought discount-store sardines three for a buck, and only the faux Oreos, and at some point must have taken a pledge of allegiance to a store-brand sugar-smack cereal that came in plastic bags so big they looked like garden mulch. We grew up on cherry pies scavenged from the day-old discount rack, their bright orange starburst stickers declaring them "SPE-CIAL!" which we eventually learned was baker-code for "PER-HAPS A WEE BIT OLD."

You pass a lot of people in the grocery store, but Dad was one you noticed; he had chia-pet hair, a ski-slope nose, and was so severely freckled that the spots sort of bled together. Then there was his smile, a sly smirk, the way it always dribbled out a little while the joke was still being built. Dad knew his power, his own spell, his gift of timing: He was a sort of Mary Poppins, only rowdier, with a rebellious streak, his presence making everything play, everything song. Which meant, much to Mom's chagrin, that many a night of KP duty devolved into dance and riot. In his defense, he really couldn't help it; he bled music, had a real chronic case of singing. He was Tony in his high school's rendition of *West Side Story* (he told me that this is when he stopped being teenage wallpaper and perhaps got the slightest bit cool); then came Spice, a four-piece Top 40 group that covered stuff like Bob Seger and Neil Diamond and eventually produced a short run of an original record, gigging at clubs, hotels, even scoring a song on Rochester radio. He had *groupies*. The kind who left houseplants on his doorstep. And when Spice dissolved—Mom not altogether upset about it—he teamed up with a female vocalist, and the two of them weekended as wedding singers for the better part of my childhood.

So when people said that "Pat was the party," it was true. Literally, figuratively, he was the ringleader. A just-add-audience comic, the laugh track to our lives.

But oh, how he swore; how he tracked mud onto the brick-print linoleum, indifferent to Mom's just-scrubbed floors; how he howled at football on TV. On Sunday nights, the Bills would score, inciting thunderous touchdown dances that were downright primal, sending the whole house shaking. He was so... human. Sometimes, my memory tries to smooth things over, to

perfect him... crop him up real nice, then pop on some hazy fil-
ter. But it's like combing a cowlick. I try to elevate him to saint
status, but I shouldn't, and I can't.

Fact is, Dad wasn't a saint. He couldn't be—not in the classi-
cal sense, not in the poetic one—for starters, because he rarely
prayed. Or at least, not that I saw. On Sundays, ever since I was
a toddler, Mom would lug me and my sisters to church, deposit
us in the nursery with all our diapering paraphernalia, and then
slip quietly into her seat. Alone. Wrestling a monkey of my own
now, I see how this was somewhat superhuman, meritorious of a
rippling red cape; she, on the other hand, simply laughs, telling us
that by the time she had one of us all French-braided and zipped
up in her jumper, the other had husked her stockings clean off.
Faith was for us girls, all those mornings; Dad stayed home and
read the swap sheet. Did the Jumble.

The few times I remember Dad calling out to God, he did just
that: He *called*. He delivered grace at the dinner table, sung loud
in Latin, all stagy and monk-like: *In nomine Patris et Filii et Spiritus
Saaaaaanctiiii.*

Then, downshifting, and marginally more serious: *Bless us, O
Lord, and these, thy gifts...*

Grace for garlic pizza, for green beans, was something just short
of Gregorian chant. In the summer, when we dined outside on
the back deck, the cantation grew louder—loud enough for the
neighbors to hear over our row of arborvitae. And some Sunday
afternoons, while unloading his band equipment from the van,
stacking it up along the far wall of the garage, an impromptu concert might erupt, his Yamaha Clavinova rendering an "Amazing
Grace" that rattled up my bedroom heat vent so rolling and rich
I could barely manage my math homework. The house would

thump with the zeal of a robed gospel choir, complete with shout-blessings, "Hallelujah!" and "Oh, sah-weet Jeezus!"

Dad found the play in everything, and for the longest time, I think, maybe even God was a bit of a game for Dad. Something to hoot and dance around, singing loud, laughing. Something to keep at arm's length, the way you can keep distance best: by making it good fodder for a good joke.

He taught at a Catholic high school, so he knew all the motions. In and out, tapping it out cardinally, on his chest, the north, south, east, west. When we'd attend Mass while in the mountains visiting family, my sisters and I were herky-jerky, just trying to mime, like we were new in dance class, always beats behind. We didn't know how to kneel, when to stand, all the great calisthenics; we slurred and mouthed our repartee with the priest, and timidly tried to offer peace, but Dad did it so beautifully, slipping into formation like a synchronized swimmer, strokes seamless, folding in. And we watched and wondered.

His family, growing up, was devout. In fact, the year before he was born, my grandparents were featured in the paper's "They Live Their Faith..." series because they did; they walked it, the way grandparents do: in the snow, uphill, both ways.

Here is where I want to be so careful, because I believe it's vain and presumptuous and, really, perfectly pointless to ever pretend to know the inner tickings of another human soul. But also: because I believe the mere act of going to church on Sunday, or Saturday, or midweek on Wednesday evening is not a good enough litmus. Church attendance makes you a Christian about as much as pushing someone into a swimming pool christens them an Olympic freestyler. Which is to say: Warming a pew by itself is perfectly predictive of nothing, except that you needed somewhere to sit. Hopefully... hopefully, it is symptomatic of a hungry heart; a faith that's thirsty, always coming back to lap up the water. A heart that knows how the world will wring you out, and wants so badly to be filled again. A heart that wants the community, all the iron-on-iron, all the smithing and sharpening. The great pack to run with, to cheer you on when you've got a cramp, or a bad knee, or are simply out of air.

That's why we go to church all those mornings. That's why we open our Bibles, and make space to pray, and pepper one another with questions: Because we need answers. We need truth the way we need road signs to navigate.

At some point I notice that other dads come, that mine does not, and so I ask Mom: *Why not? If he knows who God is, then why isn't he hungry?*

She lifts her shoulders and sighs, frowns slightly, but doesn't flinch. He'll come when he's ready, she says. She's telling me, and maybe she's telling herself. In the meantime, she says, we pray.

This is a half-good answer to my child mind, and, since I have recently met my friend Nancy Drew—and tomboy George, and pudgy blond Bess—it does what all half-answers do: becomes the greatest mystery. Dad's indifference becomes a nagging riddle, a great cloaked secret, a thick and fuming fog. I lay the clues out, and I can't fit them: how you can be nursed up on the good sweet stuff, these sating truths, and then just gather it up and pack it away.

How can you not be hungry?

I keep my ears up. Perked and ready, panning for clues. And once I learn what I'm looking for, I become somewhat better at spotting it: the hints and winks that tell me that, deep down, perhaps he is still hungry a little.

Turns out, soul hunger can sound a whole lot like music, which makes sense, when you stop and really consider it: all that reaching out and aching forward. And as I get a bit better at playing Nancy, I learn to unbutton and unmask, and it's as thrilling as finding a cipher or a secret set of stairs.

I start to see the song beneath the song.

It's there, the hunger, all sloshing around, and it's even loud sometimes, the growl: all those decibels at dinner grace, all the booming garage worship. But I find even bigger clues in the lower rumbles, the ones that come slipper-footed and soft, pianissimo even, as he perches on the edge of my bed on a school night. This is hunger, I think, as he sweeps my flap of bangs aside with one hand and, with the other, traces his thumb slow and reverent across my forehead, two lines kissing in a cross.

I bless you, in the name of the Father, and the Son, and the Holy Spirit . . .

I lay. Stone-still. Watching, waiting, for what comes next.

And then, *Amen.* A peck on the cheek.

And good night.

His finger, cool and smooth, a bit of heaven flowing. Putting some seal on me. Whatever was happening, whatever he meant, I never asked, but I'd hold my breath for a bit of magic, this commissioning always so clean, so innocent, so honest, a tickle and twist and wiggling hope that maybe. Maybe something was inside Dad, something that was still searching, and still throwing sparks. A seed, maybe. I hoped that his wanting God to pour favor over me meant that he still wanted from God . . . and that while tilling my forehead, God was turning up new earth in the deepest heart of him.

When I looked in the mirror the next morning, and drew the hair back, like a curtain, there was nothing.

No sign, just skin.

Whatever else, whatever hunger Dad still had or didn't have, it was subterranean. It was basement stuff, and it stayed there. Maybe it came up on Easter, Christmas. He sang "O Holy Night" in a way that was so haunting, it would make Ebenezer Scrooge curl up and cry in a fetal position. He'd sing, and you could see it, the reaching, the stirring...but then it all went back in the box with the tinsel and the tree skirt and Mom's homemade crochet-trimmed stockings. And so we left it alone, let it grow cool and musty, soft and damp and speckled; we learned not to probe, not to push. Somehow, like the cancer, this was something Dad was wonderfully clear about. Don't start. *Don't ask.* He didn't want us Sunday people prattling in our patent leather shoes. So when Mom sews us Bible totes to bring to Christian Life Club, the quilted fabric dappled in tiny pink hearts, we proudly swing those bags through the fellowship hall. And when I get back home, I make sure to let my take-home papers, my Popsicle-stick crafts, my memory verses spill out onto the kitchen table.

Maybe...

Mom was so solicitous, always trying to make him thirsty, always making sure to take a long, slow pull and show it was fresh, and cold, and good. She would bait and cast, toss out her line, a subtle plea. Overtures.

How about this Sunday? The kids are singing.

Or,

There's a drive-thru Nativity; we won't even have to get out of the car.
But almost always it was no. *Have your church,* he'd say, though
we told him it wasn't about *church;* but he'd brush it off, duck
back behind the newsprint, and so we got in the car and left him
there with his Raisin Bran. And this scene loops over and over so
many times in my mind, in real life, that the whole thing grows
slack. Eventually we don't fight, and he doesn't fight either, and
we reach a sort of armistice: his heart behind a thick curtain, not
meant to be probed or touched.

Every year, when we pose for our church family photo, a little
pyramid, Mom is at the apex, leaning over us, huddling big-
winged like an angel. Or at the bottom, the firm base to build on.
Either way, there she is in the middle, proud and plucky as Carol
Brady, a lovely lady with three girls of her own.

When the directory comes out, Dad's name is listed, but he is
not pictured. He is in parentheses. This is how our church family
comes to know us, and this is how they see us, whole; but to me,
we look like half a puzzle.

I tell my friends I have a father, but he stays home. They nod,
don't poke. To some, he is imaginary, like the tooth fairy. On
the Easters, when he obliges, when he quietly puts on a striped
button-down and joins us in our pew, it is like we are sitting with
a unicorn. We do the fisheye and try to watch him, sneaking
glances throughout the sermon, x-raying through the skin to see
if something is waking up, uncurling, coming alive below. How
do you know all the moves, all the words, and not want more?
How can you be so satisfied with only a sip? How can you not
want what God promises: all the sweet springs rushing up cool
within?

After the offertory, we stand and turn around for a perfunctory ten-second greeting, and the couple who practically owns the pew behind us reaches out to grab and shake his hand, and they are rabid, a full-eyed friskiness that terrifies even me. I cringe. Don't they know better?

On Wednesday nights, at youth group, when my leader opens the floor for prayer requests, my hand always slips up. I am thoroughly predictable. For Dad. And all our heads hinge down, hands squeezing around the circle, a popcorn of prayers asking that something might move and change and shuffle within: that something would unlock.

I learn to breathe them at night, too: little hiccup prayers, for Dad.

God: Just make him hungry.

My mom says she prays for Dad, too. Keep asking, she says, because it's all we can do. Well, that and live a kind of light, emit a gentle glow. Just sparkle. She smiles, points me to 1 Corinthians 7, to the fourteenth verse where she's laid anchor.

Try to be patient, to be consistent, she says. And most of all: Trust. So, even by age seven, my home is my home, but it's also become a bit of a mission field. And a stage. I am always aware of Dad's eyes on me; I am always so sure that I have to love him in an impossibly winsome way. I am convinced that all of it counts—absolutely all of it—and worry that I'll somehow spoil it. That he will see the uncut version, me unabridged; I know everything is exposed and everything matters. He will be weighing it all to see if I really mean what I say, if my faith is more than a sweet butter frosting.

If I am more than my string of Sundays.

As much as I focus on leaking light, I also feel the opposite: that I am folding in. I begin bottling up part of me. Not on purpose,

26

but I ferret out the moments when Mom and I are alone. She sits at the foot of my bed, my rose spread folded back in thirds, streetlamps low, and I ask her all the impossible things. I hand her my enigmas, because I want to know what she knows. About marriage, about dating. About a rotating cast of boys I am just moony about, about how you know.

I want to know even slipperier things, too: the alchemy of forgiveness, how it functions. What it actually changes. About omniscience and free will and how that math adds. About being patient, and jealous, and grateful. And about how you give yourself a good shake when you feel petty, and small, and unseen; how to herd all your itchy thoughts, point them in a good direction; how you come to love your weird and winding body; how you take a higher view of the whole big board game, and live on purpose, a life like chess, a mapping of your moves.

I don't ask Dad.

Not that I am cordoning him off, or because I don't want to talk, but because I am convinced that we can't.

And so, by the time I am eighteen, there are whole acres of my heart that he'll never know.

I pray for him, more. I puff prayers out like little exhales, little bubbles floating out, and up, so autonomic and ingrained they are a kind of respiration. I am knocking on heaven, ringing the doorbell. Leaving God voice mails. And e-mails.

All the same memo: Dad.

God: Dad.

Jesus: Dad.

I am bleeding my journal wet with these pen-prayers begging, hoping, weeping, asking God to call out. To be loud.

Dad has a great ear, impossibly perfect; he can play for hours. Just eyes closed, fingers dancing. No sheet, no notes.

But for the longest time, it's like there are things he can't hear. Or won't.

When I am in second grade, I campaign for a pet rabbit, and my need is myopic. Dad brings home one of those massive flip-chart notepads, the ones teachers use, and I take a smelly marker and make a formal presentation that debuts after our spaghetti: *Five Reasons Becky Deserves a Bunny.*

I produce a serialized story next: "The Adventures of Puffball," written and illustrated in thirty-plus pages. It's tagged quickly by its sequel, "Easter Made Easy." And then, bunny fever officially rampant, one of my girlfriends throws down the most epic of all elementary school birthday parties, and because she is an only child, and at that, a leap year baby, the whole thing becomes a bit of a circus. Really: For her eighth birthday—technically, her *second*—we go to her McMansion, where her parents have hired a magician. My brain just about buckles. A real magician, black bucket hat, snow-white gloves. *In her living room.* And while he doesn't pull a rabbit out of the hat, maybe there is a flapping bird, a dove; and in lieu of goody bags, she sends every last one of us girls out the door with a Jurassic-sized stuffed animal. A *rabbit.* Toffee fur and golf ball–sized eyes, it is humongous. It is better than the gift I got her, and I feel equal parts guilty and incredulous. Really, the stiff-wired ears come up past my waist.

The next week my mom and I take a late-winter walk in the woods behind our house. It's March, but mild enough to be traipsing, and I turn to Mom, midway, catching her when she's winded and a little bit weak. I move in. I look up and twinkle and ask: *If I find a bunny out here, can I keep it?*

And she says: *If you can catch it.*

For a day or so, I think this is the greatest promise, that I have it in the bag—or the hat. But then I realize how empty this is. You can't fool the rabbit reflex, those glassy eyes. They're scared and skittish, and they see everything; the slightest snap of twig will send fur flying.

I never speak it, but at some point, I presume it: I make the same ask of God. I look up and bat lashes. Plead. If I can softly, barely, hardly creep up—if I can come upon him glacier-slow, unthreatening, hands raised high, a pinky promise to be so perfectly unimposing; if I approach him by not approaching him directly; if I come at him without confrontation, from the most oblique of angles...

For years, I try to have conversations without words. I try to move in, closer, without moving at all.

I try to catch Dad, so I can drop him right in God's lap.

And I have about the same luck.

Weeks before he dies, the oncologist is overly optimistic. He tells us we have months, maybe a year. But even a year feels like tomorrow, and that puts my blood on the boiler. I'm immediately antsy, and throttle the prayers up a notch. Warp speed. I move from patient and kneeling to pacing and squirmy. And I stop leaving God voice mails. I get an air horn.

I get on my bike.

I pedal far, because the road is sort of my prayer closet, my way of getting quiet, my trick for shucking family, my way of making space.

It's June of my senior year, and school is winding down, and I rebel a little, leave my helmet on its hook and let the wind whip past my ears. I pass silver dairy barns, the air farmy fragrant, the cool sour of earth, of cows and corn. I pass wheat. I pass a church where someone has transplanted an old McDonald's playground, a hamburger prison, a totem to Captain Crook. We live in the maybe-farmland, a little stitch that's not quite suburbs, not quite country.

And I start to feel it, Dad slipping. I feel the urgency, the cool breeze running over my cheeks, and I feel so sure that we are moving toward that moment, that good-bye. The world looks too raw, that's how I know. I see the rough edges, and I feel anew the horrible heat of the fire within. For years I've been holding this torch. This burden, really: the possibility that I am the only Bible Dad might now read, that I am a girl, but I ought to be all gospel. Be text. A love letter. I am to be a mirror, a missive, a reflection, bouncing off a bit of Love, a bit of God.

And I know there is not enough of me to do it. I can't build the kind of blaze that will burn big enough or bright enough to scorch and smoke and steal his attention.

I can't be the kind of fire that will make him hungry again.

If I can be obedient, and always smile, *maybe*. If I can get in the habit of leaving my heart always gaping, wedged a little bit open, warm and inviting and eager with answers, no fear; if I can Miss America walk, with a calm assurance and well-heeled dignity, girded by the best kind of bedrock, a true kernel of worth; if I can burble up with a bit of joy that comes from somewhere else.

Just sparkle, just shine. And then, *maybe*.

My vision is blurring, I am feeling empty, and sleepy, and spun around, and a bit unsure of what comes next. I have turned this

Rubik's cube over and over in my palms, trying to line up all the tiles, all the colors, trying to untangle the trick. Trying to understand all Dad's reasons for saying no, for bowing out, for building this wall. *Why doesn't Dad want all of you, God? Why can't we walk this together?*

This feels hopeless. And so, that afternoon, as the wind rustles fields—shakes the corn, tosses wheat—I bend my head, too. Right there on my bike. I tell God, *Okay: Here's the deal.*

I lay it all out.

I am willing—I say—then I pause, for impact.

I go ahead and tell God:

I am willing to give him up now *if it means I'll get him forever.*

My legs are heavy as I signal left, cross the street, one last push up the pitch of our driveway. With the bike back in the garage, kickstand flicked out, it's then that I let go of the handles. I uncurl my fingers. This is the moment I shift my weight, one foot to the other. I slow down asking God to save Dad's body, and I amp up prayers on the deeper front: I ask God to send more munitions to his soul.

I pray hard, harder, hardest of all.

And when I have prayed so hard that there is nothing left, not even breath, not even groans, I stop trying to catch him.

And of course, that's when it happens.

Chapter Four

TIES AS TISSUES

It's so curious: one can resist tears and "behave" very well in the hardest hours of grief. But then someone makes you a friendly sign behind a window, or one notices that a flower that was in bud only yesterday has suddenly blossomed, or a letter slips from a drawer . . . and everything collapses.

—Sidonie-Gabrielle Colette, French novelist

Dad is dead, and I am astounded at the precision. Those first few days.

They should be blurry but, somehow, are crisp, creases pressed. There are caskets to consider, then flower sprays. Obituaries to craft, summing a whole life in just a few sentences. Song selection. Eulogies. A million imperatives when your mind is a million other places.

There are calling hours, a tender service, the farewell caravan slow-moving toward the cemetery.

Like dominoes, everything is lined up, black and white, this or that, perfectly spaced and set and measured. And then someone pushes the one on the end, and it begins: Everything falls flawlessly, fast—far faster than you could have imagined.

Suddenly, it's over.

★   ★   ★

Dad died at three in the morning, and ten minutes after he froze—that's what it looked like, his mouth the littlest bit open, loose-jawed, like he'd just flat stopped—we gathered a week's worth of limp-necked flowers and stale brownies, magazines and toothbrushes, and moved out of the hospice ward.

It felt wrong to leave. The place had become our home base, our fort. The nurses were *our* nurses, and the fridge in the lobby was filled with our food. Everyone brings food; grief's love language is food.

It felt even worse to leave Dad there; to push the elevator button, to sink down to lobby level, to drive away without him. But we kept reminding ourselves, for the first time of many, that this was "just his tent, just his shell."

It's hard to do.

It's hard to kiss the cheek, the tent, the shell, when, for as long as you've known the tent, the shell, it's been your dad. And then suddenly, you're supposed to start up the self-talk, the big bold believing that it's not really him. Your mind must do Houdini magic, must create an impossible schism, freeing the man from the box.

It's no small miracle, trying to believe that the body is no longer the person. So that morning, before we left, I kissed him. I planted a gentle one on Dad's cooling cheek, a first good-bye, even if it was just his tent. And whispered, near his big, long ear, that I loved him, even if it was just to his shell. It would have felt wrong not to.

We drove to Dad's brother's house, nearby, and some of the relatives stayed up for a bit longer, keeping my mom company. It was that eerie predawn hour—not quite night, not quite morning—and they were trying to laugh, trading old family memories, even so soon. They didn't want Dad to stop, I think. Not yet. Mom was exhausted, tapped dry, so wrung of emotions that she could take part, even at times laughing and shedding a story herself. That is all I remember; that night is half-clear, half-cloud. The acidity of my emotions has deepened what small scratchings the mind managed to make that day; I dare not trust my details. Most have been filled in to make the story whole, I know. Days that important cannot come piecemeal, and I've probably done a little editing with my memory.

What I do know is that I bedded down on a soft leather couch, an aunt lovingly having fetched us blankets, and drowned, swallowed in the deepest kind of sleep. The next morning—or rather, later the same one—I woke, assaulted by too much sunlight, my eyes full of scrim, and a sickeningly sweet crowd of donuts and kuchen on the coffee table.

I sat up, disoriented, and things began to register. Faint at first. The blanket-covered human lumps spread atop the other couches; the heady scent of French roast spilling in from the kitchen. Soft, tiptoe tones and nervous laughter. And all that sunshine flooding in from a set of sliding glass doors that offered a panorama of the backyard...a big backyard.

Not my backyard.

My uncle's.

I began to pet down my pillow hair, and then the thought came, socking me hard in the stomach.

This is the first day I'll live without Dad.

Something about me felt vulnerable just then; like the donuts, I had a hole in my middle. My throat lumped up, pulled tight. I stood up, and my heart felt open, exposed, like I was missing my rib cage. Like every hug might kill me.

In the other room, Mom held a pen, and was already making phone calls: to meet with the funeral director, to run an obit in the paper, to call the family lawyer. Jumping through all the right hoops. I was impressed, but shouldn't have been; she's the oldest of four and, just a few years back, had buried both her parents, barely a month apart. The funeral director had joked that he was going to start reserving a room for us.

I was leaning against a counter, watching preparations take shape. The throat knob was ebbing some, but I still hung back, desperate to blend in, afraid I might somehow look different now; that there might be a bit of writing on my forehead. *Fatherless. Half-orphan.* It felt that obvious. How could I not look a bit bobbly, scuffling around in this new skin? No matter; it was all vanity anyway. If I looked like a newborn fawn trying to stand, quivering legs and a face tight with fear, no one would say it. People were too polite to ask how it felt to have Dad dead.

Instead, they asked if I'd slept okay. If I was hungry.

Yes, no.

They didn't ask if it hurt. You're not supposed to.

Planning proved good distraction. Like lining up those dominoes, meticulously spaced, clean, all smart formation. I volunteered to give the eulogy, since I like to write. Everyone waited a moment, eyebrowed me as they took slow sips of their coffee and searched my face for the slightest twitch. *Was I serious*, they asked, without saying it, and I nodded yes, I was. I really wanted to. I'd kick myself forever if I didn't, I said. I owed Dad this much. He would want me to do it.

My youngest sister, Danielle—who holds tears inside too well, too nobly, very much like the Dutch boy who plugged his finger in the dike to spare the village—said she would sing. I was as impressed with her proposal as the rest of the family was with mine. My older sister, Rachel, chimed in now, too, ready for her part. She would read during internment, and we'd get all the way to church having forgotten her Bible and would have to borrow one of the standard-issues from a wood box on the back of a pew. For years after, the book would sit on the parcel shelf in the rear of Mom's Buick, brittled by sunlight until it eventually split, coughing up gospel like a bad cat.

At some point after, we sold the car—maybe with the Bible in it.

Later that first Dad-less day, after the first round of arrangements has been conquered at my uncle's kitchen table, we leave, pushing through a barricade of hugs, kisses, and "Are you okays?" to change the underwear we've worn thirty-six hours straight, shampoo our hair, and head out for an afternoon of errands. First stop, the drugstore. Then the mall. We need waterproof mascara and mourning clothes, and we are shopping on a deadline.

Picking a dress might seem like a bit of a relief, a bright little island in the midst of our fog, but no: Spend a late summer afternoon helping four women find flattering funeral attire—on a shoestring—and you'll see. The late-August mall is always in transition, with fall waiting around the corner, but the earth still all oven-hot. Penney's is trotting out the first towers of turtlenecks and backpacks, but they're also still selling some straggler dresses. The problem, we find, is that they are frolicky: floral, and pastel, and ruffled. They scream *wedding* or *beach* (or worse, *beach wedding*), because that's what you're supposed to do in the summer. You're supposed to amble on boardwalks in spaghetti-strap shifts while ice cream trickles down your chin and your sunglasses slip and sweat beads up on the bridge of your nose.

We try to find our focus, to find tasteful dresses, to help Mom arrange the dominoes. But the mall assaults us, bright and igno-rant, just like everyone in it. I don't know why I have never real-ized this before, why I've never appreciated the absurdity of people so eagerly trading their precious time, so happy to cage them-selves in a string of air-conditioned shops to buy cardigans and strappy stilettos and slow-wick soy candles that can't ever make them happy. For the first time, I get a little angry at a stranger, a girl whose hardest decision inevitably will be whether or not to add whip to her java-chip Frappuccino.

And I am tempted to grab the frumpiest rag on the rack.

The following afternoon brought viewing hours. I put on my dress—a black polyester wrap with a sash that, if pulled tightly enough on my scrawny teen frame, produced the slightest, softest curves. Rachel had the audacity to say it.

"Wow, you know, that kind of makes you look like you've got some hips."

She meant it as a compliment, honest, I think, because she'd always upbraided me for lacking them, for my boyish frame; she always said there was too little art to me. But that day, that off-hand remark—that sideways compliment—hit me all wrong. Like a hammer. It wasn't for a very long time later that I learned that having a little hip is good, for reasons my husband tells me are enigmatic, absolutely and inexplicably wired into the male mind.

But Rachel's comment came *before* that husband-helped epiph-any, and I might have shoved her, hard, if she hadn't been riding shotgun and I in the backseat. I cried all the way there, quietly scorning the hips that I had, or didn't have, I wasn't quite sure.

The waterproof mascara worked.

Mom put on her blinker to turn into the funeral home lot, and it was then that I remembered: I was supposed to be missing Dad. I wasn't sure just how much my eyes had to offer, and I had to ration; the tears were owed to him.

We walked in, and some other family members were already waiting in the lobby, wearing brave smiles, sauntering over to meet us, not sure how much to talk or touch. I felt like a China doll in a shop with a strict break-it, buy-it policy. No one wanted to be too rough, to get too close, at first. They kind of sidled up, soft eyes, a little "Hey, honey" hug-press-squeeze. I don't blame them for being so gentle; I was having just as much trouble knowing how gingerly to handle myself. It was like I was watching myself in a movie, wondering what was lurking around the corner, wondering what I might do next.

I knew this much: I was dreading stepping any closer to the open casket.

I was fearing my final look at Dad, dead.

Easing in, I snuck a quick sidelong peek, a flash from far across the room. I caught a toe-to-head profile, his proud nose pert and high, and I let out a breath I didn't know I'd been holding. It was him. I could move closer.

Dad, pariah of the fashion world—proud wearer of cartoon alien T-shirts, those horrid reversible shorts, pitiful sneakers (besides the rotting Sauconys, he'd recently purchased a black Velcro pair, plus a pair of turquoise Chuck Taylor high-tops that looked like he'd filched them from a Ringling clown)—who would have thought I could ever be scared to look at him now, having the calm assurance that Mom had picked out his final clothes, that he was carefully coifed in the blue suit jacket, the pants, a tie?

But this time, I was fearing something different. Not that he wouldn't look polished, primped, put together, but oddly, that he *would*. I'd been to other viewing hours before, and seen the dead look so different, bad Ripley's doubles, so yellow, overpowdered, overwrought. I worried he'd appear glossy and airbrushed, *beyond* us. Suffused with that *Touched by an Angel* halo glow. I wanted him to look a little reckless, irreverent. I wanted him to look like himself.

I know, I know—the tent, the shell.

But still.

Luckily, Dad's curly hair lent itself to few styling options; the mortuary beautician would have been hard-pressed to find a way to innovate, do it wrong. It would probably look fluffy, clean, like he'd just toweled off from a shower. And since men don't play those daily games with makeup, painting a sort of second self, any potential for mistakes there was eliminated, too.

Still, I edged closer with small hopes. After a day without him, just being in the same room felt right. The family felt whole, five for five, a full fraction—one. Wax double or not, it'd be good to be with him.

At the casket, relief washed like warm rain. I was struck, more exhaling; I mouthed a thank-you prayer. They did him up just enough. He still looked like him. And really, he looked rather nice; more peaceful, more like his healthy self than he had leashed to all the IVs, with those tired, soldiering eyes. He even looked like he had regained a little weight, a good swell to his cheek, and if no one told me, I would have sworn he was making a comeback, *thisclose* to beating the cancer, pulling a Lazarus, his greatest joke.

With his eyes closed, arms folded neatly, he looked like a man who had found what he was looking for. A man tired but happy; a man done with his search.

That first worry vanquished, another surprising thing struck— or didn't, which was the next marvel: The little knot in my throat that had tripped me up, on and off, unexpectedly during the most random times for the year prior, the whole time he was sick—it hardly had time to form. My high school friends—most just a week into their freshman year at college, and, lucky for me, most at local universities—came back and ladled hugs, dull and soft and good, like chicken soup. Checking my forehead, almost; making sure I was doing okay. We talked about where their roommates were from, if their professors were already pummeling them with papers, what it felt like to be all grown up, all away from home.

I remember feeling surrounded, blessed. Hemmed in and held up. Not lonely.

Later on that evening, in the funeral home hallway, someone tapped my shoulder, cornered me—I think trying to kindle a little hope. They short of sang about faith being a good anchor now; about the firm grip of grace, our covenant with Christ, the spoils of heaven. I nodded in all the right places, hoping my head-bobbing would help hasten the sermon. The words were tantalizing, even true, hopes I swallowed whole, but it was such a perfectly wrong time to remind me of what I already knew too well: that Dad was beyond me. I feigned interest, like I appreciated all the assurance, but inside, I was a kid wailing to be let out of the corner. Back to the milling crowd, to people who expected little and sniffed around gently, like wary patrons in the glass shop. I preferred the people who trafficked in mild hugs and the same simple questions: "Will you head right down to school, Becky?" and "Is your mom holding up okay?" Those were easier.

I remember little else of that night, save a few flickers. It went too fast. The dominoes Mom had arranged fell faster, neatly down in line, so soon that we barely had time to step back and watch. Mom looked striking in her mourning clothes. She shouldn't have looked so pretty, tawny, butter blond hair barely grazing her shoulders, a slip of rose lipstick dewy in the dim light. An old friend of hers even made a pass, hinting, so vaguely, at a date.

But for all her beauty, she was all rock. How she did it, I'll never know. She had to have been running on empty, too, maybe even more than we were. Where did her fire come from, where did she scrounge up the warmth to smile and chat and so graciously, so queenly, so patiently hug? Mother, lady of faith, her well dug so far and deep, she could drink in the driest places.

We sang "Amazing Grace," a cappella, like we would around a fire, just before calling hours ended, before they closed the casket's lid. All but our immediate family had filtered out at that point, and we got to say a more private good-bye. I had been anticipating this. I knew it would be the last time I looked at Dad with these earth eyes, and for a moment, I understood.

I felt the way he did, that day he sat drinking the lake.

It was in that instant that I realized that part of me would be leaving now with Dad. I still can't wrap my mind around this idea, that a part of you can die while you yet live; it is too big a riddle. How do you tuck a piece of your heart away, forever? How do you know what to bury? I decided to swallow the mystery, to simply let go. It felt too easy.

Just before I stood up from the kneeler, I took my finger, brushed Dad's lips a last time, gathered up a final kiss. They were

41

cold as the room, refrigerated and smooth, and I remember feeling noble for still touching them. I wanted him to know the idea of him dead didn't scare me; that I wasn't banishing him to the badlands of ghost story and cemeteries and corpses; that he would always be above all that.

We drove away, safe in the assurance that there would be one more rendezvous with the casket, closed, one last chance to parse out this part of good-bye. I relished that, hugged it tight. I didn't want the parade of hugs, the extra grace, to stop.

I didn't want Dad to stop.

Our family went out to a restaurant, after. It was late, and my sisters and I just wanted to go home, go to bed, and everyone kept trying to buy us chicken wings, mozzarella sticks, anything. They said to not worry about the price. I read the menu front to back, twice. A third time. Nothing sounded good.

By the time we got home, it was late, and I still had a eulogy to write. But you can't write when you're running on fumes, so I set the alarm to blare early, instead, and curled into another thick and dreamless sleep.

The next morning, I sat straight up. I planted my feet on my blue bedroom carpet, pulled out an old notebook, and hunched over my childhood desk—the one with whitewashed knotty pine and a blue stenciled bow—and I did the most grown-up thing: I wrote for Dad. I began to bury him with words. There was a mad energy about me, all this collecting, culling, this trodding down and juicing of memories until I was tired and stained and left with something sweet and true, something I hoped might do him a bit of justice.

It was needlessly sunny, the kind of day wasted in anything but a bathing suit. I crawled into our hot-bellied car clutching three carefully folded double-spaced pages. My mom's brother held the door, playing chauffeur; somehow, the two had agreed that Mom shouldn't have to drive herself. Not to this. She could play producer, direct the whole thing, top to bottom, choosing the flowers, and Dad's burial ensemble, and the crypt—but she shouldn't drive herself to the church.

We walk into the sanctuary, and the casket stands waiting. It's taciturn, a summery oak, lonely and shy, and now sealed shut. I have faith that Dad is inside, still asleep, still gone, as it sits atop a collapsible stand, an aluminum accordion stretcher really, and wonder why you never notice these in the movies, or on TV when all stations play the same funeral, maybe for the pope, or a former president, or the retail pioneer who left his mark on millions. The stretcher looks too utilitarian, too functional, for this moment.

Still, the church is beautiful, bright. I see my Sunday morning pulpit and know I will soon stand at it, homilize on the forty-nine-year-old man who is half of me. I will play preacher; I will be Dad's voice, saying all the big, messy things I wish I'd said while he still could hear.

When it is my turn, I climb steps, fists clenched, sucking deep breaths, calm gulps, like Mom has coached. A fieldful of butterflies awakens inside, and not just in my stomach. They are flapping hard in the balls of my feet, my fingers, my toes. One lands on my tongue. My voice shakes—it always does, at the start—but soon finds a foothold. Maybe because all these eyes are holding me up, praying me strong.

You can't sum up a whole man in minutes, but you can come at him, you can approximate him by a series of tangents. Triangulation. I tried this; I spoke of Dad from all angles.

I reamed him for the heartless slaughter of backyard woodchucks, David-style, with a rubber slingshot. They were invaders, he claimed. They had no reverence for the human concepts of plots or property, but would learn, soon enough, not to harass our cherry tomatoes.

I laughed at his sophistry with telemarketers—how he peeled apart their pitches, waxing philosophical (now, was there *really* such a thing as a free lunch?). And how he pestered the poor folks at the customer service counter: *No, I don't want chicken wire—I need rabbit wire. See, I'm keeping the* rabbits *out.*

I joked about his singing grace on the patio, the concerts in the garage.

His undying, unflagging, almost religious devotion to the dollar store.

His love of the lake.

His fishing, his fish tales, his poles that filled a closet.

In the end, all these loose ends stuck together, knotted up, clotted into something, someone, who had simply left too soon.

I knew he was not in the casket. A spread of roses lay over it—Mom's claim on him, the ribbon read "Husband" in gold foil. Somewhere, there was a bouquet with "Dad," another "Brother," several "Friend."

I paused for a minute, wondering why we all were so bent on naming him, claiming him, saying who we are burying, labeling our loss.

The rest of the service rolled on, a near-perfect mix of looking back, looking forward, almost like graduation.

We choose to bury him aboveground, in a mausoleum. He and Mom, when she goes, will be placed head-to-head. I hated that Mom had to think about this; I hated that at that same moment we were visiting her grave, too, and that she had paid in advance.

Somehow it seemed that she was prebooked, that she had already checked in over the phone and might up and leave at any moment. I wish more vaults came as single units, but most are sold two-deep, and you can't very well bunk with a stranger. Buy a double, and you can choose three ways: heads touching, feet touching, head to foot. Mom said that Papa, before he died, insisted that Grandma's feet not be near his nose for all eternity.

It is so sunny, rays booming off the clean white concrete, and we squint through this final act, this internment, and then the cavalcade is over. The hearse slips off, more to collect. We all meet up back at my aunt's for a picnic of warm potato salad, frosted brownies, a sweaty pickup game of soccer. It's important for the family to come back together, to have a little levity now, Mom says. We need other people around. We need to see that we can still laugh in this new normal.

In the afternoon heat, my aunt's backyard is a broiler. So I take a cousin up on her offer, borrow a bikini, and go swimming. And I learn, firsthand, the hard way, why one should not swan-dive in one-size-too-big bottoms, especially while swimming with boys. And especially, one should not spend that degree of teenage embarrassment on a dive that, according to the lawn-chair judges, is worth only a seven.

We are pressed out, empty, as night falls. All the dominoes, down. What is left is a crackling bonfire, a dew-wet bag of marshmallows, all gluey together, and a dark car ride home—this time, the ban lifted, and Mom can resume driving.

My cheeks are sunburned, my stomach full of potato chips and pistachio pudding salad, and that's when I realize: I have forgotten to be sad.

No one has mentioned Dad missing.

★   ★   ★

The next day was the first day of real life, reentry, and here's what I wish someone had warned me: That's when the hard part begins. The parlor, the service, the picnic spreads lavished by loving relatives and church friends, they're cakewalks. They're scripted, almost; formulaic. They're dominoes. You clasp hands; you consume hugs; you say "Uh-huh," "I know," and "We'll be okay." You read the tags on the tribute bouquets; you poke at carnations and lilies and snapdragons; you sniff their severe and sad-smelling perfume and see who sent what. You brush a cheek, brush a tear, say a prayer. You sing hymns, you eulogize, you nurse the littlest, runtiest bit of hope. You leave the casket to the undertaker, you take a deep breath, you drive away.

But all the while, you are trying to stay strong yourself, because they're watching, because you're onstage. And it's not too difficult, because everywhere you go, all is *full*; the to-dos are long, the arms are eager, there are nervous, thin smiles, the world dripping with sympathy; it's almost tangible, you could almost eat it with a spoon.

But the morning after.

All the dominoes had been placed, all had fallen, and we weren't quite sure what came next.

There was nothing else to arrange.

I'm upstairs in my bedroom, folding laundry, making piles for the drive down to college. I've got a rotten attendance record already—I've just gone and skipped my first week of classes—and I'm moving, numb and slow and on purpose, like I'm swimming in honey. The house hums quiet, and that's when I hear it, the sniffling. Coming from down the hall.

I walk into my parents' room, to the corner closet, and push open a pair of louvered doors to find my sister, sixteen years old, looking small, like she's six, huddled right there on the floor. Indian-style. She sits next to a pile of ties and she pulls one up close to her nose, breathes in deep, and then looks up, pink eyes pooling.

"He's never coming back," she says.

I stand for a moment, then kneel down next to her, silent, panning for strength. Trying to be the big sister. I reach for a blue paisley tie, supple in my hands, and lift it up to my nose. I breathe.

It is Dad.

And the waters burst.

I sit all the way down and we're mewling like kittens. Sniffing, sniffling, eyes closed, conjuring him back. *Come back.* But he doesn't. We rub our eyes and keep looking down, wondering what in the world has happened.

A few minutes later, Mom is at the doorway.

And she does something I don't expect of her, our trusty skipper.

She sits down, too.

It's only moments before Rachel finds us. And sits. And all four of us women are there on the floor, squished into this closet like the tinned sardines Dad keeps—kept—in the cupboard. Someone's tears dribble onto my bare skin, puddling just north of my knee, and I don't bother to brush them off. I let them dry.

No one speaks for a long time.

Finally, Mom looks up, wipes her eyes, and swallows hard, as if to speak. We wait to hear this, because we need her hope.

We need her strength. We need Mom to champion us, to be our rock, our wisdom, our last parent.

"You know, girls..."

She starts, and then the tears are there again, the words snag and choke.

And she nods, hard up and down, agreeing, even though we have said nothing.

"Girls, you know, this sucks."

There it is. The brilliance of my mom, my eloquent mom, and all she can muster is the unladylike word we girls are never supposed to say.

I reach for another tie, a green one. We are using them like tissues.

Chapter Five

HOLY MUD

Jesus wept.
—John 11:35

My mom.

High school cheerleader. Youth group mentor. Art teacher. The kind of parent who, when we were in grammar school, spent Christmas Eve morning baking a Happy Birthday Jesus cake, and, on Valentine's Day, used to cut our peanut-butter-and-jellies into hearts and stir food coloring into our thermoses, tinting our skim milk pink. A mom who'd stayed up all night sewing coordinating floral jumpsuits for us girls to wear on a plane flight to Florida one spring, so we'd look like walking Monets at the airport; a mom who'd nailed "road signs" to the spindly pines in our backyard forest, naming wending paths in our honor: Rachel Road, Becky Boulevard, Danielle Drive.

I suppose, looking over this little résumé, you'd have expected her to have offered some pom-pommed pep talk, peppering us with verses about God planting hopes firm, numbering every hair on our heads, knowing every hurt that heavied our hearts. Perhaps she had some pretty comfort in her back pocket, an amulet, waiting just for the perfect moment; something about Christ, his holy tissue dabbing the dew from our eyes. Maybe some chilling and haunting and holy whispers of a world with no more death. Or morphine.

But no. We girls sat, famished for our war cry, and instead, we got a lament.

"Girls, this really sucks."

I wondered—at that moment—if she, as a woman of faith, had the right to say what she did. If she—if *we*—were entitled to the full dirge and dejection. If we had valid license to roam around in despair.

Was she—were *we*—really welcome here? Free to wander these cold wastelands? If we only had even a morsel, an atom, a thin and hot filament of this little-big thing called faith, wouldn't we somehow believe ourselves right out of the bogs? Shouldn't she know and trust that God could, and would, redeem this, too?

Because isn't that how hope works?

I read once that when the ocean roughs up, when the waters get all vexed and choppy, the smallest sand dollars will open a mouth hole that's under their bellies and actually swallow big grains of sand.

Imagine: Sand dollars, in the grip of a storm, eat the earth out from under them.

Sand dollars eat sand.

Maybe this is how I want my faith to work: as a consumable foundation. A mass I can imbibe, tucking down deep inside; something leaden against the kicking current. I want belief as an anchor, a ballast, a deadweight. Something sure.

Because isn't that kind of the whole point?

Shouldn't faith rinse the hurt away, faster? Clean out the wound? Wouldn't God kindly microwave Mom's grief, our grief, hasten this season, if we all tamped down, if we impelled ourselves forward and worked to be obedient, to listen, to resist crumbling, to fight the current, to do the hard work of daily hope?

Just eat sand. Just more sand.

For a while, I worried Mom's words that morning were better suited to someone *without* belief. That labeling our situation bleak was a flagrant breach of faith.

Now I realize: That wasn't the case at all.

It turns out, Mom's an emotional savant. Always has been, always will be. And that's why, rather than giving us daughters a call to arms, she did the much harder thing: She called us into hers.

Her empathy freed us to hurt. And by sitting down alongside us, I see now: She wasn't showing weakness. She was actually mirroring Jesus, God's own Son, who forsook his throne to sit down in all the messy closet moments of this sin-broke world. Maybe Mom was just daring to do as he did: To be with us. To drink from our same cup.

I now realize that it doesn't matter who we are, how wonderfully big and bushy our roots are, the ones that sweep low and feed our faith. It doesn't matter how hard we believe for, boast in, or "cling to" what God promises, because God doesn't want Velcro; he wants honest hearts. And the more I look, the more I see that even the most devout and historicized Christians have admitted to banging so hard on heaven's door, grasping for the help so frantically, that in panic they nearly drown out God's answer.

Jesus knows this pain. And John's Gospel encapsulates it, traps it in amber, holds it high to the sun so we can see. He makes sure it's a moment we'll never forget—a sniffling-in-the-closet, snotty-tie moment where even the leader, even the king, even the rock is pierced by the gravity of the stillness, the silence, the hurt.

He arrives in Bethany, late.

Late to the funeral of a dear friend; a funeral that might have been but a near brush with death, had he been on time.

Martha—history's favorite frantic hostess—runs ahead to meet him at the road.

"Lord," she pants. "If you had been here, my brother would not have died."

No hello. No "Oh, it means so much that you've come all this way." Just pure, unchecked emotion. The words almost fall out of her mouth, the way Martha's words always seem to.

And for Jesus, those words dig deep, cut in like barbs. They're words that will echo for millennia after.

"Lord, if you'd only been here..."

Jesus pauses. It's so typical, towel-shaking Martha, the woman to worry about timing, logistics, who should be where, when. Planner Martha, hardworking Martha. I'm-doing-all-the-work; tell-my-sister-to-help Martha.

"Your brother will rise again, Martha—" Jesus begins.

"Oh, I know," she heaves, runny nose, sodden cheeks, and it burns, because she believes it, believes it deep.

And yet.

"But I'll see him when everyone else rises, on the resurrection day."

Jesus bends down to meet her eyes, rubbed red. The lashes clump together, wet and sharp, like little spikes.

"Martha. I *am* the resurrection and the life. Those who believe in me—though they die like everyone else—will live again. They are given eternal life for believing, Martha. Do you trust this?"

She nods, chin sinking, beginning again to cry. "Of course, Lord...I have *always* believed it...I've *always* believed you..."

And she turns, hurries back toward the house.

The words were true. But the truth wasn't balm enough, not in her hell. Not in her frail human form, where the river of hurt rushes fast and high, and the comforts of religion seem barely capable of taking the edge off.

Mary, seeing her sister return, stands up at once.

"You'll have to excuse me," she tells the mourners. "I need to go."

Jesus is *finally* here.

She throws open the door, picks up her hem, and runs; she reaches him and falls at his feet.

Always at his feet.

And, while her posture is different from her sister's, her words, remarkably, ring exactly the same.

"Lord, if you had been here, my brother would not have died!"

Where were you, God? What held you? Why would you delay your rescue; why wouldn't you come through the one moment we needed you most?

Is it strange that both sisters—the busy-bee and the foot-sitter—would blurt out identical things? The same honest, wounded blame?

I don't think so.

That question's still shaking, even today. Maybe the wording's shifted some, maybe we've freshened things, but the complaint at core: It's timeless.

Same old story. Same plot, nothing changed but the names.

You could have, but you didn't. Isn't this the great, rolling charge? Isn't this the blight of belief? The gap in God's résumé, the grand wrinkle? Right here: Martha says it. Mary, too.

You could have, but you didn't.

This, this complaint—this delicate matter of doubt—it's the ever-active fault line of faith, earthly hurt driving hard against heaven's hope; the two slipping, scraping, shaking all the time. Two worlds, coming together, and it's a friction that devastates, that severs and quakes, that cracks clean through the best foundations.

You could have, but you didn't. And for many, it's enough; it's the deal-breaker. Why would a good God—an able, omni-God—all-present, all-knowing, who covets his people's prayers, who delights in the mundane details of their lives, who vows to be the perfect provider, to always meet their needs—why would a God who tends to the flitting sparrows, who lavishes on lilies and fusses over flowers, why would he not be the superhero we needed, rushing in right when we needed him?

"Lord, what took you so long?"

"Where were you, God? The one moment it *actually* mattered!"

"Why didn't you? You could have, and you didn't!"

"God?"

"God!"

Jesus asks to see the tomb.

"Lord, come and see." Mary stands up and starts to turn, showing the way; other mourners trail behind, ready, again, to help the sisters grieve anew.

The sisters take a few steps, until they sense that Jesus isn't following. A glance over the shoulder, and they see the unthinkable:

Their teacher has buckled at the knees. Sunk low. He's kneeling on the ground, head bowed.

He has paused to weep.

Hands wring his eyes as he heaves holy tears, salty rain pitting the earth. The crowd waits for a moment, stunned silent, not quite sure what will come next.

What can it mean, if their rock, their king, is struck down, crying, too?

Mary moves closer, not saying a word. Martha's mind reels, doing math.

Why would this miraculous teacher, their Lord, prefer to mourn when he could heal?

What kind of God steps barefoot onto the shards, the pain, when he can blot any disease?

What kind of God weeps when, with a mere word, he can still waters, shush wind, will the world as he wishes?

Whatever the reason, we have the luxury of knowing more of the story: more than Mary and Martha could have, anyway. We have the full panorama, the great gift of hindsight, of knowing how the drama weaves up and the ends all come together. We know that it's the same kind of God who would shoulder a cross when he could have kept his warm spot on the throne. It's the same kind of God who would put skin on—stretch nerves on—and entertain plenty a bruised thumb as a craftsman's kid, hunger and heat as he fasted, the dredge of dishonor and gossip in his hometown.

I suppose, it's the kind of God who craves our companionship, who longs to know us intimately, *Immanuel*, to be with us. Feel with us. One who's willing to taste the swill we swallow, day to day to day.

It's the kind of God who knew he had to ache, as we do, to show us that he really understands, that he really has weathered it, that he wasn't speaking fancy or figuratively when he promised he'd stick with us, a breath right beside us, within us, through the storms.

He's the coach who ran with the team.

The friend who broke with them.

The high priest who'd been there, too.

The whispers begin.

"See how he loved him!"

"But hasn't he opened blind eyes?"

"Couldn't he have kept Lazarus from dying?"

Jesus rubs his finger under his nose. He swallows, stands up, shakes off his cloak.

"Carry on," he says. "I'm right behind."

Mary and Martha move ahead. This road has become so familiar in such a short time. Back, forth, their grief has soaked this line of earth, tear-mud trodden by slow-shuffling sandals.

"Lord, come see," they say and point ahead, to the limestone hillside, to the cave carved, blocked by a stone.

Jesus tugs at his sleeves, loosening them.

"Let's roll it away."

"Roll it away?" Martha gasps. "But Lord, it's been four days!" Her nose crinkles, incredulous, as she lowers her voice and leans in, a loud whisper. "Lord, think of the smell!"

Jesus chokes on a laugh—he must have. Martha, still so practical.

"Didn't I tell you you'd see God's glory—if you believed?"

Martha cocks a brow, interest piqued but still wary. She squints. Studies him.

Then she takes a deep breath, steps aside, as men lay hands on the rock and start to push.

The rest of the story is history, literally. Jesus calls Lazarus forth (perhaps humoring Martha, who could hold her breath only so long and wouldn't dare risk the odor of actually walking *in*); the mummy-brother walks out, is unwound, sloughing graveclothes, cold skin gaining color, coming supple in the sun. And the story ends, the Gospel flows on, full-sail, somehow leaving more questions than answers.

How did Lazarus feel, his spirit summoned, stuffed back into a stiff, small body? What sort of publishing offers could he command for first rights to tell his "Four Days Dead" story?

And I want to know: Where did the sisters run first? Did they clasp the brother who'd come back, or the God-man, who, if slightly late, deserved the glory?

But my biggest questions always circle back to those tiny beads of holy mud, heaven's tears, back on the path, drying down to dust.

Why would God—in full knowledge of his impending miracle, absolutely aware that Lazarus was mere minutes from a bravura performance, from being beckoned back—why would he still stop in the middle of the road to cry?

Perhaps he was troubled by the sisters' doubt. Maybe it bothered him that they thought him insensitive—an impenetrable, shelled-off God. A removed, distracted teacher, burdened with better things to do.

Maybe it hurt to see the women feeling so forgotten, so small.

Listless, defenseless, overlooked.

Empty eyes, low on hope.

Or maybe it was just what it seemed: His dear friend had fallen ill, had suffered, had died. Death's known for its sting, but that's a euphemism; death is downright venomous. It paralyzes, blisters, burns. Yet he reached, fingers wide, and took the cup. He tipped it back, with two hands, right alongside the women, drinking the same doubt, the vertigo, the disbelief. The hollow rot in the heart. He swallowed this cocktail, all of it: the shriveled hope, the hovering fog, the not knowing what came next or how to pick up the pieces.

Still, maybe it traced further back. To Eden. Maybe it pained him that paradise had come to *this*. Earth, a planet predicated to hum on perfect love, was now a stew of loss, lust, lies. Sin had slithered in, full of fiction and filth; the whole place was septic. At every turn, there was snarling, the weary groans, the whispers of his indifference, hints that he was always holding something back.

Really, how good can this God be?

Maybe his mind was even a little bit anxious, already tasting a bit of his cross. Maybe it hurt to know that the nails, the sword that would be sunk into his side, the mocking thorns shoved down—the hell, the darkness, and the way his Father, for three days, would turn his face—all those things would square eternity, would save people from dying twice.

But they would still have to die once.

They would have to do the bravest thing imaginable: They would have to lose one another. And in those moments, they would suspect his goodness, his sovereignty, the surety of his promise.

They would suspect him, himself.

And maybe, in a very real way, that hurt.

I don't know where this idea comes from, but we're trained to grow up believing that grief can be smoothed over quietly with flowers, headstones, hymns, and Hallmark.

That if we tiptoe around grieving people—if we channel our energy into feigning strength, so they can be weak—somehow, this will help people heal.

Even I had originally expected this in those moments when I wanted more from Mom: better advice, more rock, more faith.

But oh, what a fib; faith has never been the inoculation for tears. Even the God who knew the end of the story would stop in the road to weep. His pausing, his taking time to let his heart fall freely, isn't that proof enough?

That we have a right to cry? That we have a right to drift here, into these parts; these eddies, this grief? Don't you dare tell me different.

I distrust the sincerity, the true understanding, of anyone who tries to help me leapfrog over the pain, the roaming, the tears.

I suspect any person who offers me a Kleenex before a shoulder or a shirtsleeve.

Or a tie.

Chapter Six

SORTING LAUNDRY

"I know the plans I have for you," declares the Lord, *"plans to prosper you and not to harm you, plans to give you hope and a future. Then you will call on me and come and pray to me, and I will listen to you. You will seek me and find me when you seek me with all your heart."*

—Jeremiah 29:11–13

The August that Dad died was the same August I began my freshman year at Grove City, a small, private college in northern Pennsylvania. Partway between Erie and Pittsburgh, it was unexpectedly preppy—a "ring by spring" school, where you could covertly matriculate in marriage. When weather cooperated, some girls clicked to class in heels; boys layered up sweaters in a style I can describe only as Nantucket.

I was excited to start. Mention it, and I was effusive. I had picked out a set of jersey knit sheets and a matching comforter, all in a blue sky pattern, and taken everything out of their packages, spreading them over my bed at home, imagining, then refolding and rezipping them back into their plastic sheaths. I planned to drive down wearing the world's most inspired pair of faded bell-bottoms, fluted with fine faux-leather piping along the back pockets, and the last few nights, to be sure I didn't forget it, I even started storing my still-wet toothbrush in the pile stacked beneath my bedroom windows.

Maybe this is selfish, but in the quiet of my heart, in the safe space of my journal, I gave the thought full room to run: I moaned. I told God, more than once, that it seemed awfully inconvenient that Dad was starting in on his final descent, planning to land right as I was packing life up into cardboard boxes, plastic bins, laundry baskets. I look back and wonder how I could have been so intent on this, so tunnel-brained, so blind to bigger things. But I was: I was wonderfully young and impatient and couldn't see past my own nose, head all up in my cloud comforter.

Part of it was that I was the first kid on my mom's side to go away to a four-year school; the other part, and this is vain: I thought I'd really earned it. Two months before, I'd graduated tip-top of my class and delivered a blustering valedictory address about, what else, *the big brave journey*; about being dauntless, about being present, about putting your toes up on the dash and hanging your hand out the window and just enjoying it, thrilling at every hairpin turn in your story. About soaring wide-winged, about believing in your own electricity, your own beauty. About taking time to do the hard digging, sifting through your ingredients, untangling how you were made, and then lunging—hard, fast, forward—into whatever big magic came next.

And *that*—that is why, secretly, I expected a little more fanfare. Maybe a care package, but the cookies were being deflected to the hospital waiting room.

I feel callous admitting it, but I wanted to go. Looking back, I almost don't understand it; I don't see how there wasn't more conflict in me, more wrestling. But this is hindsight at work. In the thick of everything, my journal reminds me: The hospice ward was exhausting, and a diversion sounded divine. I didn't know if I could take many more days cloistered in that small, rosy room, bisected by the big metal bed, dizzy with the lazy-Susan good-byes; I didn't want to keep making more memories watching Dad half sleep, face rippling in a little grimace as he drifted in and out, a tide, ebbing away in his thin blue gown, stomach swollen with cancer. Wouldn't these be the first days I'd try so hard to unremember?

Life was still happening outside the hospital, and I wanted to live it.

I wanted orientation, that first chaotic move-in scene, the one you see in the movies: upperclassman boys with big grins and thin T-shirts hauling love seats up three flights of stairs. The first fizzy sips of four years of free soda. Everyone watching everyone watching everyone. I wanted a fighting chance at the bottom bunk; I wanted my due part of the commotion. I wanted the circus, all of it, twittering and tingling as all that newness met and pooled and bubbled over in one tight minute. Like driving a brand-new car off the lot, this wasn't something you could just pause, rewind, and replay, and as a girl who too much craves blank canvases, the newborn smell of spiral notebooks, and squeaky shoes, *this* was something I could not miss. Having me give up my move-in madness, those first days? That would be awfully cold-blooded of God, I thought.

Especially on top of the fact that I was already giving up Dad.

The day before I leave—before my aunts drive me down to school—Dad is in bed, half sitting up, maybe 60 degrees, and somehow, still smiling. Having lost so much weight, the grin sags, like it is draped from two pegs hidden deep in his cheeks.

I don't know where to begin my good-bye, so I ask if he needs more ice chips.

He doesn't, thanks.

We sit, and we talk about all kinds of wonderful nothing, skating soft on the surface. Like I am tracing the same figure eight on a frozen pond, looping it over and over, like I am too scared to make my jump.

I sneak my eyes to the clock and think, *How do you do this?*

How do you say a big good-bye, disguised as a small one?

I reach for his hand, the one not tethered to the IV, and we sit a few moments more, quiet. The room is so pink, so fuzzed and lit by white light, it is like I am sitting inside a seashell, and I am clean out of words, because sometimes there is nothing and everything to say, all at once. His hand in mine, it feels like I'm cupping a bird: light, veiny, thrumming, like it might fly away. And I hold it, loose and hard, both, and hope and pray that all my unspeakable words will flow through the tips of my fingers as they press into his palm; that they'll seep beneath his stippled skin and into the big blue rivers, be ferried back to his heart, and then: Then he will know everything. The unsaid everything from the past few months.

Few years.

My digital camera warms in my lap—a graduation gift from him and Mom—and I nod to it, say thanks again. I promise to capture lots of shots of school, as many as the memory card will hold, so that I can bring them back, show them off to him, hold them up proud, like fish. *I caught these!* We've both heard rumors that the campus is almost obsessively manicured—the central quad so lush and leprechaun green that kids are forbidden to walk on it—and we've mocked the absurdity of it, imagining sentries stationed around a precious plot of grass.

Grass.

We talk a little more, about my roommates. I have two, coming all the way from Colorado and Washington State, and the
three of us make a *triple*, which is just Grove City doublespeak. It
means we'll be crammed into a room built for two. Dad says he
hopes the girls are as good in person as they sound on paper; he
insists that I call soon to let him know how everything is.

And then, he tells me to go. He wishes me luck and, foremost,
fun. I tell him again about the big first-night graffiti dance, where
the freshmen shimmy into white T-shirts and shake hands and
autograph one another with Sharpie markers, a rainbow rat's nest
of ink, all those names, all over. Like a walking yearbook. It is
Grove City College legend. I have packed three tees, just in case.

He listens, again, and grins.

And then I lean over. I kiss him.

If he had asked me to stay, I know I would have, in a heartbeat. But
he didn't. Dad made a big deal of my going away, and I'll always
thank him for it. Looking back, I now realize how absurd it was that
both of us would play along; like my little dart down to school and
back amounted to a big, dramatic farewell, like I was the one leaving.

What a gift, him setting me free.

At that point, we didn't know if we had days or weeks. I was
absolutely itching to start, but also serious about dropping it all,
stopping on a dime, and speeding the three hours home when
he was getting close. I meant it. I pressed Mom, made her swear:
She would phone me the minute he took that turn. I would rush
home, because I wanted to be there.

With that, I planned to treat college like two tidy bookends.
I would start school, pour a wet foundation for friendships, find

a groove. When Dad was ready, I would hurry home—I would do all the brave things, I would walk that dark, dank valley—but then I would also have something to return to, in Pennsylvania. New rhythms to slip back into.

I spent those first days foraging for books, meeting hall mates, spreading that illustrious cloud comforter, pulling it lake-smooth over the top bunk (I was last to the room). And I was inundated with everything, just as I'd hoped: a torrent of fresh faces—students, professors, cop-like cafeteria ladies who short of frisked you for filching an apple. New buildings. A new laptop. A new Walmart, replete with new navigational challenges in finding the VO5 shampoo and strawberry Pop-Tarts. Already taking shape were little cohorts of lunch buddies; sororities and fraternities had begun culling the freshman class, wild for new blood, and before lectures began, there was all the leaning over, saying hi. Cursory résumé-swapping. Everyone sizing up everyone else the way you paw through melons at the grocery store.

All these experiences, they whet my tongue. And they would soon call me back for more, offering a dizzying itinerary of things to try and learn at a time when I otherwise might not know what to do next. This was my plan, my prescription; what my health-care career, so many years later, would teach me the real name for: *prophylaxis*, a kind of medicine swallowed ahead. The funeral would be a blip on the screen, and college would bring me "back to our featured program." It would give my world a drumbeat; a song for my feet to keep walking.

I made frequent phone calls home those first days, between the ice-cream socials, and skits, and that first-night dance. I kept checking in and asking how Dad was faring, if it was time for me to head back, if we were near the end.

On the third day, my mom said that a trip back home wouldn't be such a bad idea. Doctors said Dad was rounding that last corner. That he was almost ready.

My aunt made the drive to fetch me, sweet woman, suffering a seven-hour round-trip to haul me home. I don't remember what we talked about; I think we were both just praying, under our breath, that we'd get there fast enough. And we did. We made it. Dad died before dawn, but I got my real good-bye; I got to stand there, part of the small circle around him, before being properly engulfed by the funeral whirlwind, the dominoes, and that terrible, tie-sniffing morning. It all came and we filed through it together, in step, as neatly and methodically as anyone can. Clean, precise, dexterous, like we were threading a needle.

Then it came time for me to head *back* to school. I felt selfish this time, but I was grateful, too, like a little girl in a one-person lifeboat, paddling away from a wreckage, fast, for fear that its sinking force would suck her down, too. Maybe just being back there would help me heal. A holy distraction, a well-timed mercy. This, I thought, was God's favor, finally shining. Miraculous, this provision, his wings. *I could hide here*, I thought. *This is my cleft in the rock.* And I hugged my mom good-bye on the graying brick stoop in front of my all-girls dorm.

And she started to cry.

And I decided, right then, it was my turn to be the rock.

For about a week, it worked. Schoolwork had stacked up while I was away, and I fought piles: I was four calculus assignments and two chemistry labs behind. I forked over an obscene amount of money for the few textbooks I hadn't had time to find used— textbooks my professors might or might not actually deign to use.

I collated syllabi, carefully plotting my grand catch-up plan; I begged sweet strangers to trust me as I borrowed and copied their lecture notes. I recited the same "I'm sorry I'm late" speech to professors, again and again. *I really am in your class*, I'd say. *And here's why I skipped your opening act.* I tried not to be too theatrical, too wilting, and they, in return, were collected and mannerly about it.

In the margin—and there wasn't much—I made feeble attempts to wire myself in socially. I tried to make friends and be vulnerable and do the bold, big reach, but it's amazing how quickly cliques congeal, setting up almost overnight, like Jell-O. This was a world not quite yet infested by cell phones; my roommate had bought an adorably obnoxious red Pottery Barn phone, romantically retro with the rotary dial, and I pulled out my USA Datanet calling card, winding and winding and winding round all the numbers, paying 99 cents a minute to patch my way home and make sure everyone on the other end was doing okay.

Grief burrows into your bones, whether you give it notice or not. Despite a schedule bursting at the seams, and little time left to whimper or weep—despite plenty of chances to trade fake hellos, polite grins—I felt emptier each day. I kept my tears and sadness tucked away, only to be indulged the moments when I was in bed, lights out, turned toward the white concrete wall. Or on the phone. It could not be let out when there were strangers around, strangers whom a breakdown would inevitably alienate, terrify.

And really, this grief—my father—was something far too precious to be synopsized and presented to them. It would not fit a book jacket flap or an abstract. The whole story was too long; the whole loss, too dimensional; the emptiness, too full of big feelings to explain. I didn't want to reduce it to a quick sketch. That seemed laborious, and it seemed disrespectful; it seemed cheap. I needed arms that, when they hugged back, were actually hurting along with me; arms that implicitly understood the man who was missing, without so much as a word.

I needed hugs that were as hopeless as mine.

Could I find it here? I wondered. *Could healing really happen, this far south?* And how? Wouldn't it be wrong to demand hours of ear, counsel and care and unconditional listening from someone I had barely met in the bathroom while brushing my teeth? Someone who, between frothy mouthfuls of peppermint spit, had managed to tell me only that she was from Ohio, lived three doors down, and was majoring, tentatively, in biology?

Pour my heart out, to who?

I made an appointment to see a counselor, like Mom suggested. Then canceled it. Cold feet. I turned inward, noble with my secret burden, my catching up, my heavy backpack, my heavier heart. People asked if I was doing all right, and oh, I know they prayed; kind strangers, who brought stuffed animals, and carnations, and filled my mailbox, *Thinking of You*, but each day grew harder, still. We were all there, freshmen, all relearning our world; but I was also relearning how to inhale. Exhale. There was that quiet, creeping consciousness that I was becoming a little bit of a martyr, my grief a cilice no one could see, a constant scratching against the skin. This was the hand I was dealt, but I didn't quite know how to play it; I couldn't find a way out of the mounting pride of my own pity, the prison of my own hidden hurt.

The breaking point came one afternoon as I heard groups of girls giggling, skipping down the hall and off toward the cafeteria, passing my door swinging their ID cards on those maroon Grove City lanyards that everyone bought at the bookstore. All I could think about, from way high up on my bed, my seat in the clouds, was this: It would be so impossible to skip right now. And that's when the clarity came.

This was not a time to dance, or skip.

Grief is not gregarious.

This isn't going to just go away, not here.

As the laughter dissolved down the hall, I realized: That closet moment had finally found me again, two hundred miles south. Grief, that thirsty bloodhound—I thought he'd lost my scent, my trail, but no—he's a professional, he's trained to track.

I couldn't keep running.

I called my mom and asked her if it would be weak for me to give up now and postpone my start. What if I took a semester off? What if I pulled out to glue the pieces back together?

She told me no, it wouldn't be weak. It'd be a pause, a break, not quitting.

"I was hoping you would," she admitted. "It was too hard losing two at once."

She later told me she had asked her Bible study group to start praying for my coming back home. She knew, even then, how much I needed it. And with all those godly women rapping on heaven's screen door—believe it: even one named *Faith*—I now see that this decision was mine and not mine, all at once.

I was all too eager to leave once I had Mom's endorsement, and right away began boxing up the laptop and printer the school issues every freshman. I found their cardboard boxes still in my closet, and I began squeezing them back into their Styrofoam and schlepping them back to the technology center. I removed my clothes from their hangers, refolded them, and apologized for purging and unplugging my mini-fridge; I walked over to the dean's hall, pacing nervously in a cave-like waiting room, unveiling my plans to an administrator who offered only a pinch of pity, then began moving the papers that would earn me a partial refund, walking papers that would let me leave. I relinquished my ID card and meals next, too soon, stomach growling; I foraged for fruit snacks and corn chips and fake grape juice in the vending machines down the hall. I sat on my top bunk, spread my junk-food feast out on my stripped-down mattress, and hoped Mom would show up soon.

Coming home commenced a quiet unlike any I'd ever tasted. There was no homework, and my dearest friends were hours away, rightfully consumed by their own college careers, and the rest of the family had a schedule. My younger sister was in high school, a junior; my older one still lived at home, but woke before dawn to fry donuts and pipe flowers onto birthday cakes at a local bakery. And Mom: She lived the staccato of substitute teaching, using her free days to rake the house, tying loose ends—helping Dad die to a telemarketer, *I'm sorry, sir, he doesn't live here anymore*, blotting his name from a bill, smudging him out from the basement laundry room with each folded pair of underwear.

It was down there, helping Mom switch loads late one morning, that I realized how right my decision to stop school had been. I looked around the basement. Butted up against the east wall, there was an old navy couch so loved and so sunken in that it was spilling its innards. And everywhere, all along that couch, and on the floor beside it, rolled small foothills of socks, slacks, shirts, all proof of how our rhythms had stopped, and how foolish my plans had been to try to simply bulldoze ahead.

Clearly, something had happened. There was wreckage here,

in this basement heaped high with Dad's clothes, washed, dried, and folded from his final wearings. These were the clothes Mom had tried to put away, tuck back into the drawers, with little luck. They wouldn't all fit. We soon realized the problem: The flow of laundry, in most homes, operates under the same hypotheticals as the economy.

Most money itself is only an idea, always changing hands, always flowing. *Currency*. Your IRA isn't sitting in a silo full of coins, Scrooge McDuck–style—which is why, if every American decided to cash their accounts out in copper so they could, I don't know, *take a daily swim in it*, we'd fast uncover the secret: It's *fiat money*. Which is a fancy way of saying it's a say-so system that works not because it's fixed, or actual, or implicitly valuable, but thanks to mere agreements in men's heads.

Which itself is another fancy way of saying this: We're off the gold standard.

That was the same problem, we found, with the closet and clothing drawers standards. Those, too, were not fixed things, but more of a grand idea for our family, notorious for our laundry room, hampers engorged with whites, darks, and damp towels. Life is motion, life is laundry—and so, when the time came to liquidate the space in Dad's tall ebony dresser, all the hangers in that terrible little closet, it was not enough. His T-shirts blubbered out over the edges of his drawers—we could knead them under the lip, punch them down like dough, and try to shimmy them shut, but then...then they might be jammed forever. Eventually, we gave up, making piles on the floor, right there in the basement. Sorting. Winter jogging sweats, and summer shorts, a stray pine needle still in the pocket. His jeans, so embarrassingly Swiss-cheesed, poked full of breathing holes, like his bait bucket. There was a box now, too, full of baseball caps, and argyle dress socks, and silly novelty socks—the Christmas tree pair that played "Jingle Bells" if you pressed a button buried in the hem—and a few lucky ties that had escaped becoming tissues. Then I folded one particularly disastrous T-shirt: gray tie-dye, starring a motorcycling Martian with a ripe lime head and leather jacket. And I laughed, and groaned, and that helped the walnut welling in my throat.

We called his brothers to pick through, to take whatever they wanted. And then we bagged the rest, drove it to the nearby Salvation Army.

That laundry traffic jam stuck with me, though. I kept thinking about it, sensing that there was a bigger lesson here I was not grasping, one I couldn't grasp at the time. Years later, I've realized: It was too great an analogy for grief. In my mind, in my heart, perhaps there was only so much room. I could hurt only so much, reminisce only so much, at any given moment, and then I would have to wring my hands and shake it off, distract myself with something else, get outside for a cool walk or bike ride to clear my head. The heart's a sieve, and sometimes there's just too much to sort through.

I would need time. Time to cup and cull memories, and there was no way I would be able to do all of this precious sorting at school, away from family. I would need to hold things up to Mom, and ask: *What about this one?* And we would frown, and fold, and sigh, and then decide.

Or sometimes, decide to decide tomorrow.

To fill the spare hours, I took a job as a pharmacy tech at the local grocery store. I learned far more than I wanted to about my neighbors, grade school teachers, classmates. I knew which moms medicated their whole brood with Ritalin, and who was drinking the dregs of depression; who was trying for a baby—or adamantly *not* trying. I learned that, at least in my experience, pharmacists were chronically cranky, undercaffeinated people who spent their days scanning orange plastic vials, dispensing counsel to china-boned old ladies, passing the best part of the afternoon in one cramped corner, a swirling sea of small pills with long names. I learned that customers can be curt and snippy with a teenage girl behind the counter when an insurance glitch declines a payment. "I'm so sorry," I'd say, broken record. "I'm afraid you'll have to take it up with your TPA." And they'd huff off, muttering threats to fill their lovastatin elsewhere.

At home, grief kept doing her work, rewriting rhythms. We were admittedly disoriented, a little touchy. A quiet undercurrent of anger, despair, wistfulness set in, and in the safe haven of our house, we named our losses, unflinchingly, out loud.

"We used to eat dinner together, before Dad died," someone grumbled. "And we'd say grace really loud."

"We never grill anymore."

"We're lucky if even the grocery shopping gets done."

Somewhere around this time, we realized our swimming pool was on the verge of collapse, and Mom insisted that we do the kind thing and put it down. When the men finished, they left a giant pockmark of sand, which later gave way to crabgrass, and the whole disaster looked apocalyptic, like we'd been blasted by asteroids. Or alien fire.

Like we were losing.

"The backyard looked better, too."

We grew bolder. We grew blunt. Holidays, time, it was all tagged accordingly: "the first Christmas without Dad," or "his last family reunion in the Adirondacks," or "the last Myrtle Beach camping trip," or "two summers after he died." His death was our watershed, like the famous Continental Divide zigging through the Rockies, commanding all western raindrops to the Pacific, all eastern dew to the Atlantic. Memories, traditions, and patterns, they were all relegated to great oceans of "before" and "after"— perhaps better named "then" and "now." We didn't realize how much we were labeling our losses, orienteering in our new life without him, but we were; we dog-eared holidays not by the gifts we gave, or got, or the inches of snow that fell, or didn't fall, or the first time Aunt Barb brought her first heavy, homemade cherry cheesecake, or the first year she did not. It was Dad. We marked and counted everything by having or not having him.

I know that this, in many ways, makes great sense. It's an old idea. The calendar itself schisms with the arrival of a baby Savior, history parted by this holy invasion, stacked up neatly into great walls, before Christ and anno Domini. Grand arrivals, like shattering departures, have a way of drawing so much attention that they become epicenters; all meaning swells from them, from that hinge moment when something swings and breaks expectations, good or bad. No one leaves unchanged. And that moment calls attention to itself over and over again in our conversation, so much that it becomes a most convenient, most important landmark, a North Star by which all other constellations take their places.

This idea might have escaped me altogether had I not overheard Mom say it on the phone. I don't know who she was talking to, but she was trying to make some sense of it all, and she told whoever it was that death does that, slices right down the middle of everything. It bothered me that Dad had gone and split our memories, our normals, cut them clean in half and left us alone to make new ones. And it annoyed me, a little, that Mom could talk about it into the phone so frankly, as if this were our lot, as if we had nothing to do but learn it, live it.

But she was right.

Again.

My job at the pharmacy was only part-time. Twenty-six hours a week counting and recounting amoxicillin, funneling drugs into childproof vials, was not nearly enough to distract me. *20 pills. 90 pills. 120.* I was restless; I was a jetliner waiting on the tarmac, grounded by technical difficulty. Bad weather. I was George Bailey, mired in my own Bedford Falls. Moody about it, too. There were great lulls and deafening quiets when I drove home from work, or before I left for it, or even while I was there, lost in the monotonous cadence of count, pour, twist. The weather turned cold, and soon even those long, nowhere-bound bike rides— something I was dangerously fond of—were out of the question.

The first few months after Dad died, no matter what we did, were doomed to be one long, drawn-out closet moment. We gave up and gave in, the earth moving beneath us, caught in the hinterlands of varying work schedules, varying dinnertimes and dinner company, varying moods of loss, freedom, gratitude and anger, emptiness and bursting, and even with God, varying cycles of Edenic intimacy and desert wandering.

I would be lying to say it wasn't dark.

I poured hours and hours of ink into my journal, wondering what mattered anymore, what I was made for. What did it really mean to have *God* as a father, and for me to be his daughter?

I wondered about school, too—particularly my big and vaunted plans to study chemistry, *to go forth and do something*, and how I had snap-decided that so instinctively, the way you grab a box of breakfast cereal down from the cupboard. The more I ruminated, the more I journaled, the more I was convinced: I didn't really even like chemistry. I wanted what chemistry could provide. I wanted a secure and respectable job, access to a nice assortment of niche ideas, the kind of mind-bendy stuff that plays well at dinner parties. I wanted to broadcast my brain like a pair of geek glasses; I wanted to wear the relentless suit of the scientist, the pretenses of a lithe and insatiable mind, ever asking, ever testing, never quite sated. And—if I can be completely honest—I simply enjoyed the way the major, now declared, had sounded. It had such heft to it; it had earned me approving nods from people whose admiration I coveted most.

But then I thought of Dad, and his funeral, and all the kindnesses paid to his dead, deaf ears, and I knew that all great eulogies are never heard. It doesn't actually even matter what people think, because when you die, it's an empty ovation; it's flattery paid to a tent, a shell.

Dad had ruined me for earth's applause, disabused me of any good vanity, any hopes that I might find any real joy in parading and performing in front of people.

When it comes to your critics, there's only one. And there are only five words you long to hear.

"Well done, good and faithful."

Almost manically, I began dusting for fingerprints—the ones I knew were all over my life, that are all over everyone's—and I questioned what, exactly, it was that God had fashioned me for.

I knew that, whatever it was, it would be something that electrified me right while I was doing it, not in the moments after.

I wanted an honest labor, true to the shape of my soul; one that I could work at, panting hard and heavy, a good sweat; one that brought a bath of endorphins, the thrill of being completely alive and completely exhausted all at once. Whatever it was, in the end I wanted to have breathed so much of myself into it that it became my *art*, alive as much as I was.

I didn't find that in science; I'm not saying people can't, but I couldn't. Part of me has always been romantic, relishing an apt word, the glint of a good metaphor. I'll be forever fascinated by the notion of minds meeting in great writing. Time travel, telepathy,[1] it has been said, already happens in books; thoughts bloom eternal on the page, intimate and instant, stories shared without so much as an utterance across centuries. And don't get me started on the pure power of ideas, how they can be absolutely infectious, and a good book a willing vehicle for revival or epidemic. That potential—the promise that matter and motion can be unlocked, unleashed by the perfect combination of words—has always won my greatest fear. I have held authors to the strictest standards. Their influence, this thought-leadership, is a divine burden, something to be stewarded; it is not a scepter.

In this lull, in the wake of our Great Divide, I asked God to stir within me, to show me what I had been made for. I was ready to live differently after Dad died than I had before. I was ready to grant God more dominion, more claim on my time and energy. I told him that. I invited him, begged him even, to invade the pause and speak into the silence. I told him I could be patient, too, and maybe that was a bribe, a bit of a game, a try on my part to not look quite so needy; if he chose to keep being silent, I said I'd wait. That I'd use the margin to let my mind mull over these big ideas a bit more.

He called my bluff. He took my offer to be quiet and more ink flowed to my journal. But in the midst of that stillness, in my effort to trust, my mind was still racing, working deeply, untying knots, wild for clues. I was worried about my inertia; I was sure that without formal schooling, with so much time counting— literally counting—medicine, my mind was turning into oatmeal. Within days, I again grew fidgety, my pious patience wearing thin. I began to ask God, again, to show me, *show me*, where to go and what to do. I began to do this loudly—one-word groaning prayers, just calling his name.

I remember the exact moment I *knew*—the day I finally made sense of the fingerprints. Sometimes God shouts, sometimes he whispers, and sometimes? Sometimes he just expects us to get practical: to look ourselves straight in the eye. One morning, November, stone-cold and gray, I was blow-drying my hair, and the epiphany came. Like rain sloughing chalk doodles clean off the sidewalk, I got honest. I got over myself and my pretense, stared right into my unmascaraed eyes, and nodded. *Okay.*

And I admitted that I was a great deal more interested in books than I was in beakers.

All the high school lab partners I've ever had will agree I'm a somewhat sloppy scientist. I perform experiments a little too casually, the way most people cook—a pinch here, let it simmer another minute there. I have no great passion for significant-digit data, for the rigor of producing the perfect pink titration. I don't like wearing splatter coats and goggles, or the clumsiness of working with fumes, shielded by the glass as my hands stretch out far in front, fumbling under a hood.

What I liked about chemistry was its math. There's orderliness inherent in it, deep principles running through; it's a language you can learn. For a while, I thrilled at the immutable rules of how matter moves, how molecules behave under standard heat and pressure. I tucked them away in my pocket, squirreling facts the way some people used to amass Beanie Babies. And I really liked learning them. There was the formula for fudging a liquid's freezing point, helping it limbo lower—and of course, a recipe for the reverse: making it patient, slow to boil. Master one, then two, and the concepts start to stack and lock like Lincoln Logs; polarity, electronegativity, solubility, the ballet of acids and bases: It just makes sense how certain atoms, thrust together, are prone to perform. You learn how electrons ring around them, priming their personalities, and the world unravels before you; you see its underbelly, and everything starts to make too much sense.

Because I was fascinated by these principles, these imperceptible rules and relationships that help earth hang together—not the redundancy and precision of test after test at the bench—I wondered if I might be better suited to another idea field. One more forgiving to a clumsy hand.

And the answer was almost too obvious. Who would have known that all the times I reached for my journal, asking for direction, railing against God for his earsplitting silence—that this, the litany of questions—they were the answer the whole time?

Well then, go: Use your words. Kick your legs around a little, but write honestly. Seek me with all your heart, all your soul, all your mind, all your strength, all your words.

It's adorably ironic, now, to admit: I was just short of begging God to write a message on the wall, and go figure: The answer was right there in the question.

Write.

I have always been a bit of a scribbler, someone who can't really fully untangle what she believes without wrestling it out on paper. At age seven, I would wake at 6 a.m. and sit alone at the kitchen table for an hour with a soggy bowl of Rice Krispies (generic, "Crisp Rice"), a pen, and my flimsy-lock diary, recording school bus conversations and second-grade afflictions with a great sense of duty. I entered essay contests, and often won; once the judges gave the prize to the runner-up, so sure my mother had meddled with mine. I got a handshake in the hall and a water bottle, instead.

On the weekends, I wrote books for fun. I read poems at family reunions. I even "published" a handful of nonfiction titles, swaddling them in dust jackets using Saran wrap and a stapler.

The writing has been a life raft; slippery, sure, but something to cling to. It's given me a chance to slow down, a lens to look longer, more closely. Writing, as Anaïs Nin so perfectly put it, is just another way to double-dip, "to taste life twice." It's a chance to examine, test, and weigh, rummaging all around inside our world, ourselves. And isn't that also the job of science, in its broadest sense?

And it fits me. The pleasure it produces, it's hardwired in. I love nailing a sentence or turning a phrase the way a skater loves a clean landing on a triple lutz; the way a hunter beams after his bow finds an eight-point buck. Sure, it's a quieter art, no crowd flinging bouquets on the ice, no wooden lodge wall to mount it up on.

But I love it.

In that rawness of the Dad-less pause—in that obnoxious but beautiful hush—I decided that writing would be one of the few things I would ever truly be happy doing. And I was learning that true callings come only once—maybe twice, if you're lucky. And so that November morning, I picked up the phone, held my breath, and dialed.

And Grove City said that yes, there was room for one more in my new major.

And like that, I declared: In January, I was heading back.

Chapter Seven

NEWTON FOR NEWTON

When my heart was grieved
and my spirit embittered,
I was senseless and ignorant;
I was a brute beast before you.
Yet I am always with you;
you hold me by my right hand.
—Psalm 73:21–23

My older sister is obsessed with amusement parks. She is in her thirties. She will sit at my kitchen table and recount every roller coaster she's ever been on, where she sat, how bumpy it was, how fast, how high; she'll debate whether it's more terrifying to have the uninhibited view from the front car, teetering over the edge of the biggest hill, or the full-speed of the caboose, as everything else yanks it down.

But it's not just the coasters. Her passion for parks is total: the log flume, and the Ferris wheel, and the swings, and the bumper cars.

To counter her, I hate the latter; I hate the electric poles running up the metal ceiling, the annoyance of the cluster jams, four or five cars snarled together. I hate the guarantee of a good collision from an angle you least expect. Who in their right mind would pay any sum to strap themselves in for two minutes of ramming and a complimentary headache?

Truthfully, though, that's almost how the first year or two without Dad felt—like I'd been buckled into a nasty game of bumper cars, condemned to a congested slog through the motions, life's circles and cycles, round and round and round. And then, occasionally, when I least expected it, *bump.*

The memories hit me: head-on, sideswipe, barreling from behind.

The first came at a wedding later that fall.

One of my mom's college friends, another art major named Shelley, was getting married fresh out of school. Mom had gone back to college at forty-one—one of the reasons I'm convinced she'll be perennially hip—but Shelley was barely brushing her twenties, making her just a few years older than I was. Dad was gone a month now, maybe, and Mom decided to bring me as her date, not wanting to go stag since she only really knew Shelley, not her family, not any of the other guests. I, not having much else to do besides bottle pills at the pharmacy, happily tagged along. I like weddings.

The ceremony and reception were bundled together, held at a town park just a few miles outside the suburbs. It was a fiery fall day in late September, and our high heels had a hard time spiking across the grass. Walk, walk, *sink.* Shuffle, shuffle, *sink.* We pitched our weight forward, out onto our sweaty toes, following the faint twang of country ballads to their source: a CD player and set of small speakers stowed in the rear corner of the pavilion.

The shelter was modestly decorated—maybe a few of those white tissue-paper bells that fold out into honeycombs, the ones you hang from the ceiling, and a lacy wishing well for cards. A small army of tea lights quivered, casting sheen and glow on the thin plastic table-cloths that covered the picnic tables. It wasn't the glossy magazine-spread wedding I'd always dreamed up in my mind, profuse with flowers, the head table a mile long, wispy and white and effulgent, a room dripping with chandeliers, a fountain bleeding chocolate over bananas and berries. Still, it was sweet in its own way, humble and honest, a wedding unbuttoned a bit, reclaiming its very roots: a bride and a groom and God. Mom and I found our place at a long table and set down our purses and waited patiently for the introductions, toasts, the penne and meat and sauce. Spongy slices of chalk white cake, and coffee and first dances.

First dances. Until that moment, I had forgotten all about the traditional dances—especially the tearjerker where the father gets a little choked, dazed and drippy, as he dances with the princess-daughter he's handing away. As he meets her eyes, there's that look of longing; it hits him: His baby has gone and grown from girl to woman, and he's worried. He's being brave, but he's nervous. And happy. And sad. More emotions than men are built to process, and all over again, you can see: It's like he's boarding her on the big yellow school bus. It's like he's uncupping his palms and finally setting a fledgling free.

Shelley was adorably short, and she had to get up on tiptoe, almost, to ring her arms around her father, and in that moment I realized how little I knew about her, except for the details Mom had casually leaked about her paintings, her projects, her nonchalance and unplanned humor. That Shelley lived here or there, that she preferred acrylics to oils, or maybe the other way around, but really, that was all. She was caricature; she was playing a role for me. I didn't know if her dad had taught her how to ride a bike without the training wheels, and had scooped her up when she tore down her first real hill, caught a tree root, and fell, the ground knocking the wind clean out of her, leaving her lungless, so sure she would die. I didn't know if her dad told the most chilling ghost stories, or extolled the virtues of a perfectly roasted marshmallow, or could revive absolutely any song on his guitar. Had he taught her how to stab a writhing worm onto a hook? Unthread it from the fat lip of a fish? Had he told her, when she first met this boy-man, this husband, the one standing backed up to the wall, that he was not worthy of her, that no one would be?

It was the treacly dance, one that's practically rolled in sugar, so designed to pull tears and sighs out of onlookers with its tale of youth grown wise and free and ready. Like that *Fiddler on the Roof* song, "Sunrise, Sunset," the dance motioned finality and freshness. The bittersweet trading of one man's shelter for another's.

And it was a dance that, though I knew next to nothing about Shelley, or her father, I still felt the full weight of. Mom and I caught each other's eyes, and knew.

And for both of us, very quickly and very tenderly, sharp, and in an instant, Dad died again.

It was not a royal wedding, or needlessly coifed, but still, I was happy for Shelley, envious a little, even. I know, because envy claws at your throat, quickens the pulse, and when we drove home that night, car quiet, moon low, I felt it: like a hand at my neck, the fast breath, the simmering in the stomach. Envy and happiness, all sluicing together, and I had a strong suspicion that perhaps I knew how lucky she was, maybe even more than she did.

That wedding, that dance, was one of the first big bumps I didn't count on, but it wouldn't be the last, not by any stretch. These bumps came again and again, in the stupidest ways, the most irreverent places. One morning, fetching a hammer from the garage, I found myself sitting on the wobbly wood stool near Dad's tool bench, digging through shallow bins of nails, and wing nuts, and bolts all mixed together like metallic fruit salad, wondering what in the world he was using as an organizational scheme, if anything. Then another, a year later, finding a half-used bottle of Barbasol in the motor home's medicine cabinet as we emptied the rig for a quick sale. And always, while riding my bike and catching that first whiff of charcoal, someone outside cooking hot dogs—because, for some time after he went on, the grill was forgotten, and family dinners became a fend-for-yourself free-for-all, an endless string of peanut butter sandwiches.

Bump. Bump. Bump.

Slowly, with each little knock, I began to itemize my grief: I began to find and count all the sore little ways things would never be the same. And these moments, this loss, would keep crashing into me, and I into it, more and more undependably. Life became a never-ending round of bumper cars, and mine had a jammed seat belt.

No one warned me, but people do not die in one day. Yes, there's something for the death certificate and the county's vital records, the inscriptions on the tombstone, but those are just technicalities, really. Dad kept dying in little ways, not just at the usual land mines—Thanksgiving, Christmas, that first unsung birthday—and those little losses were surprisingly poignant. Every forkful of pasta was not his famous macaroni salad, and I missed the garage door opening on Tuesday nights and hearing the keys jingle in one hand while he balanced a steaming box of pepperoni pizza in the other.

I missed the pantomime he incited as we hand-washed dinner dishes, the kitchen dancing sideshows that got my mother all irked, so wonderfully angry; I missed the corny Valentine's Day cards (a bulb glowing, *You Light Up My Life!*) and the very cheapest box of chocolate candies, the waxy kind with caramel centers so tacky you'd worry about losing a silver filling.

Even a few years later, at my first real job, helping to manage public relations for the children's hospital downtown, I handled a fluky phone call from a man who, it turned out, had attended private high school with my dad. And pole-vaulted with my dad. His daughter and I had jumped together, too, back when we were in high school, and my dad had always egged me on to beat her, giving me intermittent reports of her progress so as to inflate—or attack—my ego.

I remember setting the phone back in its cradle and, still flushed by the pure coincidence, I wanted to pick it back up and relay the irony of the whole thing. Immediately, I thought, *I have to tell Dad*, but then remembered: There was no long-distance carrier that could connect me to him. The excitement curdled. The importance of this old friendship, this small-world moment, would have been lost on my mom, my sisters, and even, when I got home, my new husband, who tried so hard to feel the incredulity of it all, but could not.

That moment, married, grown-up, Dad died again.

Sometimes, in those very first days, when the grief was still wet and pink and impossible, when my eyes were still adjusting to the light, I'd try to brace myself for these moments. You know, catch them before they caught me. I tried to make a list of the land mines, places I would expect the soft aches and stomach pummels, these big Dad-less voids. If I could anticipate them, maybe I could blunt their blow.

I started with the holidays and family reunions. I ransacked our time-loved traditions, looking for ones with him at the helm, and found only two: a man to scale the ladder, gussying the gutters with colored lights; and Saint Nicholas Day—an old German custom, in which we'd set our shoes outside our bedroom doors, and Dad would stop at CVS to fill them with cinnamon gum and Tic Tacs and chocolate kisses.

Then I got along to lesser traditions, those everyday moments that somehow seemed even more sacred—like riding shotgun in his dune buggy, candy apple red and ridiculous, laughing as other drivers honked. Challenging him to push-up competitions during a quick commercial break. Having a guaranteed bike ride companion whenever I wanted, and watching his smile split wide as he sliced and salted the cucumbers he'd babied all summer. How he'd tell me, true or not, to take one, that cucumbers bring you good dreams.

And then, I fast-forwarded, moving further ahead. Shelley's wedding had been instructive, and I didn't want to learn the lesson twice. I rehearsed in my mind the many times down the road that I could most expect to miss him. The birth of my nephew, who would have been his first grandchild; my college graduation and winning that first job; watching home videos and hearing his voice resurrect; one day, having kids of my own; publishing the first book I always told him I'd write.

The list went on and on, and I thought I'd nabbed them all. But you can't, no one can. To list every way someone's life has woven itself into yours? Impossible.

★　　★　　★

One night, I'm scratching around Mom's sewing room, on the hunt for a safety pin, and I pause to marvel at the closet Dad made for her, carved out of the corner of her craft room. I am realizing now just how much they built together; walls sledged out, walls shimmed in, the sketching of so many napkin-back dreams, all those trips to Chase-Pitkin. And as I turn the handle, swing open the door, and step into the thicket of her hat boxes and Rubbermaid bins and all her Sunday dresses hung heavy on the bowing rod, I remember the line from the home movie, a DIY video diary they filmed way back when the closet was only a skeleton, fresh-framed and still wanting Sheetrock. And there's Dad: I see him standing like Samson, arms palming the sides of an opening he's roughed in for the door. He's peacocking, all snowed in sawdust, as the tape rolls and Mom pans and gives proper reportage, ticking off a row of *one, two, three, four, five* new two-by-fours. And that's when Dad juts out his chin and cheeses a grin and smolders, "Count 'em again, Laurie. *Six* studs."

Yeah, Dad's everywhere. Pounded right into the walls.

And I keep on smacking into him. And oddly enough, the more I do—the more I rue these bumper-car moments, these cruel collisions, all the dying again and again—the more physics class comes to mind. Newton's third law, especially, assuring that for every action, there is an equal and opposite reaction—in layman's terms, that bodies in motion enjoy interconnectedness. That they're interwoven. That when you slam on the brakes, the brakes slam you, each action countered and balanced by a distinctly opposite motion of equal magnitude. Force for force, newton for newton, life mirrors and echoes, a thrust and parry.

And so the more and more Dad seemed gone, the more ways he was missing, the further he drifted, the more he died...the more the memories railed into me, and the more my heart learned the hard art of holding ground and holding on and shoving back.

I see now—so many years later—the bumps were not the symptom, but maybe the cure: that each moment, each memory was pulling me back toward something broken, life reopening my most delicate wounds. Like surgery just to sanitize, or a procedure to reset a poorly healed bone, and maybe that's how it all works. Maybe time heals you only by whacking you so many times in the same spot, and, sooner or later, it all starts to go wonderfully numb.

And if that's the case, then maybe these land mines aren't actually things to steer around. Maybe all the jostling, the rough ride, was not delaying my journey; it *was* my journey. It was part of relearning the map.

The British, those fancy pants, have a better word for funfair cars. They call them "dodgems." They're bumper cars, sure— same electric poles, same sorry fate—but clearly, the name suggests the value of playing a little good defense. What's more: To avoid litigation, some United States operators actually post signs warning riders to follow a circular path and avoid jamming into others. How much this is enforced varies, but clearly, it's no secret: Life runs a little smoother without all the pileups.

But again, Newton's law booms back, saying something beautiful about the way God has ordered this world: *Objects have bearing on each other. Energy cannot simply be lost.*

And that's how I know: I can't duck grief, no more than I could have avoided the trap of loving Dad in the first place. Despite what the Brits might hope, no, you can't dodge it. Because life after loss is not as simple as leveling out an uneven cake, or steaming wrinkles out of slacks, or coaxing a yo-yo back into sync. It's much messier, lumpier, sloppier. It's the car with sticky brakes; the lurching stop and start and stop again. And sometimes? It's not being ready to come back into rhythm, not for a long time.

Chapter Eight

A ROSE FOR A THORN

Each heart knows its own bitterness, and no one else can share its joy.
—Proverbs 14:10

I set out to write this book several years back, realizing that what I said in casual conversation—about grief, about growing up, about losing my father—struck a chord with other people. And after a while, enough of those conversations seeded a silly thought: I honestly began to believe that losing Dad had been instructive, a kind of trench-earned authority, enough to admit me into a sort of special club. I thought that I had a kind of insider access to the hearts of other people—other young people who'd lost parents, sure, but really, even more broadly: to anyone who limped along, aching.

Once you are part of this group, you just *know*.

But then, again and again, loss after loss, I realized how little I actually understood.

A close friend miscarried, and I had nothing. I thought—I thought I'd find the right words in my back pocket, but what was there? A little dryer lint, a gum wrapper, and a lot of wordless nothing. She told me that she didn't know how to feel, that she sensed a dull hurt but couldn't legitimize giving herself permission to go deeper, to find the pain. I sat there slack-jawed. Silent. What to say? I had read lots and lots, well libraried my grief, but I had never been pregnant at that point; I had not yet felt the swift thump of new life, just under the skin, a tender tickle in my own body, the weird and wild hope of holding part of me in my arms; and I'd not yet felt the way the same adventure can leave you, too soon, like a guest excusing himself from the table, a dream slipping quietly out the back door. I imagined that it felt like an early spring snowstorm, battering the azaleas' first pinking blooms, but I didn't dare say it. It probably felt nothing like that.

And this would happen, again and again. Early on in my career, practicing public relations at the local children's hospital, part of my job included ghosting donor appeals and writing "miracle stories"—or working to sweetly shoo away media who sometimes panted and begged, a little too breathless to speak with the teenage shooting victim, or the preteen with cancer, or genetic anomalies, or the fragile heart. My job, sometimes, was to work with parents whose baby had died, or was dying, interviewing them as empathetically as possible, pretending so hard that I understood.

How I tried. How I tried to switch shoes, slip in, understand. But I was stone. It all seemed surreal. Children, to me, were resilient, strong, effervescent. Two-legged smiles. They fell down, wailed like banshees, but then always got up, dusted it off, and got going again. At the time I had only a nephew, and knew: Children were rubber-boned and rolled with punches and laughed and lived forever.

I had no idea what it felt like to have your own flesh—your child who, in your parent-mind, is immortal—die.

Especially, before she's born.

And the stories kept coming. Tragic tales I couldn't wind my mind around. Suicides, construction accidents, slick roads. Paralysis, fatal sports injuries, drive-by shootings. House fires, botched surgeries, dead batteries in carbon monoxide detectors. More cancer. Gobs of it. And I came up short. Dad's year of winding down, one day at a time, seemed a luxury by comparison. Whether or not I actually said it, I'd had the chance—the time—to ask all the questions. To yell and beg for God to stick his finger in and intervene. I'd had a chance, too, in the midnight of my heart, to begin to envision life without him, even before he was gone. Not that these mercies made it painless—it still hurt plenty—but it was a downright opulent good-bye, from a survivor's standpoint. I know that, looking back. Mine was a clean, neat grief, lined up against these monsters.

For a while, I paused at this chapter, thinking I'd run into a wall. One built of brick, a mile thick, garrison-guarded, go no further. I set it all down at this part; I stopped writing; I was becoming so sure that autobiographical accounts were somewhat mawkish, weepy, that they only pulled a reader further down, adding the author's load to their own.

And who needs more to shoulder?

Then, one day, I realized that this wasn't a wall at all; it was the whole point. The whole horrible, exhausting point. It is twisted right into grief's DNA, and it's the reason grief is such an arduous and impossible burden: Because even when swarmed thick and tight by well-wishers and concerned confidants and the prayer-cover of your church, you ultimately bear it alone.

The loss is yours. All yours.

I have a friend named Rose.

She is one of those people with caramel eyes that always look wet, sharp, alert, and at the same time, soft—like they're melting. She asks a million questions, almost spits them out, brisk and quick like a hen gathering the morning's gossip, but somehow, she really remembers what you say, she really cares. She leans long across the table and follows up on that thing that was dogging you last time, even if there are years between your latte dates.

In this day, the word *friend* has been plasticized and, honestly, perverted; it's gone and become a verb. You *friend* someone. *Friends* is a hackneyed headcount—we play Facebook like kids used to swap baseball cards; you have this many now, but three are still pending.

So let me get a little more technical: For most of high school, Rose was what I'd consider a second- or third-tier friend. If first is the sort where you open their refrigerator, grab a gallon of milk as if it's your own, and knock on their front door more for the sound effect than actual permission—and if second is the sort you'd invite to a backyard campfire or a birthday party—then Rose was third. We'd always known each other, peripherally. We were happy to be buddied for a Spanish class project, to chitchat here and there, and she knew my mom from the time Mom chaperoned the school choral trip to Italy, when my older sister sang for the pope. But that was it. I had never called Rose on the phone, and I didn't know where she lived—at least, not until the day of the barbecue.

It was one of the last weekends of senior year, and my family had stopped by Churchville-Chili's annual chicken dinner, a Sunday evening picnic on the hillside overlooking the school's gravel running track. Families shook out old blankets, tied their light spring jackets around their waists, and chewed on drumsticks and coleslaw and warm macaroni while laughing, breathing out a bit of relief. You could almost taste summer.

Through the grapevine that afternoon, I'd overheard that Rose's dad wasn't doing so well, that he was likely in his final weeks. Cancer, too, like my dad. At that point, Mom and my sisters and I were all under that safeish (and overly generous) assumption that Dad had six or nine months, maybe even another whole year. But Rose's dad was running low. He had a month, maybe two, and it seemed unthinkable on that perfect afternoon, spring sidling up and saying hello to summer, a smack on the cheek; it seemed impossible that her dad might or might not make it to her graduation. That he wouldn't see these same leaves grow ruddy and burnt and then brittle in the fall. It seemed so imminent.

I don't remember how it happened, but that afternoon Rose and I had our moment. We started to talk. Deep talk. Talk that sliced like a hot knife through all the butter, and we got busy, heart on heart. When her dad died, I went to the funeral home, and it was like leaning over the prow, a terrible preview of what was coming. And then, a couple of months later, she came to the funeral home to hug me. And then we both moved back home from college, back into our kid bedrooms, though she was going to a local institution, so she didn't stop classes, she just quit her dorm.

We exchanged phone numbers, kept in touch. One or two nights, we met at a nearby sundae shop that's renowned for serving Goliath-sized cones (a kiddie feeds two—a large, maybe Luxembourg). We would talk, trace a long lick around, then talk some more about how our families were adjusting, or not; how maybe we thought we felt; what we wanted to do about school; why we were making certain choices—all without any need to offer tidy boilerplate, reasonable explanations or apologies.

We covered ground, lots of it. Lots of it not pretty. And we didn't flinch when ugly and indecorous words like *dead* and *body* and *widow* weaseled their way into conversation. We just kept licking. To a degree, we simply understood; we could tunnel right down into the cellar, that grief, and skip ceremony. It was humid for September, and my hair frizzling—Rose's is perennially luscious, so curly already—and our soft-serve was melting, a furious dripping, and our hearts were volatile, active eruptions. But none of it mattered; we weren't aiming to impress or act polished. We were two girls hanging out. Hanging on.

We had a couple more things in common, aside from losing our dads just weeks apart. We were both one of three sisters (she the baby, I the middle)—which meant we now lived in homes completely awash in estrogen. And we were both big talkers, gals without boyfriends—without the distraction of standing dates— and we were both pretty willing to wear our hearts on our sleeves. That made for good math, adding up to a considerable amount of common ground, not that we always felt the need to talk about it. Sometimes we just couldn't. But if we wanted to, there was the sweet assurance of understanding, which, really, was everything; the explanation and exegesis had become so tiring. All the same skirting questions, the same soft probing light. Handing out the same shopworn and scripted responses. It was nice, with Rose, to hang it all up and just be me.

The fine details of those nights have gotten muddy, grayed with the patina of time, but the conversations themselves were never the point. There wasn't anything either of us could have said that would have amounted to any sort of battle song, something brave to live for, to die for, because it wasn't that sort of talk. There were no revelations. No surprises. No advice. We were the blind leading the blind, both novices in our grief; we weren't there to educate or to glean. At that point, we were admittedly a bit cynical that there was any wisdom to be had, any solutions at all. I, in a place deep down—in a place far off the main roads, a place reached only by foot—was beginning to hope that maybe this was a time-will-heal kind of wound. And Rose, I think, was sticking with her opening argument: that this would likely handicap us forever.

In a way, we were both right.

The impression that comes back when I recall those summer nights is this: a calm comfort that came from knowing that someone else in this world—someone my age—could, to some degree, actually understand. Rose *knew*. Rose knew the confusion that clouded my home and the questions that I woke up to every morning. Maybe this was providential, or maybe it was fluky, but oh, it was amazing grace: My thorn had a Rose.

We were so lucky to be messes together.

Rose knew what it was like to stare at her dad's car in the driveway, knowing he'd parked it forever. She knew what it was like to be haunted by memories of him gaunt and skeletal, like you could see through him, a kind of frail no girl should see in her dad, a kind of frail that'll make your skin crawl. Ask any girl who's seen her dad's sunken cheeks, her young, forty-something father being helped to the toilet; it knocks the wind out of you, seeing your daddy hobble. Leaning too much on your mom's arm as he's shuffling. It's hard not to feel the throat lumping up as you try, days and weeks and months later, to shoo those memories away, banishing the bad thoughts and instead imagining him strong and striding, princely in his new body. Him walking head high, eyes forward, fixed firm on God.

What is indelibly impressed on me, whenever I think of my

Rose, is that there was someone who didn't know my dad, and who didn't know me as dearly as my first-circle friends—but she, at that moment, knew me maybe better than anyone. We were half-orphans now; we had been promoted, gone from kid to adult overnight. It felt like we deserved another diploma, a bigger one, to mark our graduation into the big bad real world our teachers had always warned us about. Rose and I had a connection, something innate and unteachable; we shared an undercurrent. A fear, really, because we knew the secret: that no one was safe or sacred, that anything could happen at any moment. Rose knew; I knew. It was a secret we couldn't hold against other friends for not having, and something we hoped they didn't have for a very long time. But it bound us that summer. She had walked where I had walked. She had felt what I had felt—in her own way.

I know not everyone has a Rose. I realize now, looking back, how ironic our situations were that summer. The timing was rigged, I'm sure of it.

The truth is, I had hardly any conversations with anyone else. Not my aunts, or my cousins, or my closest girlfriends. Just with my sisters. Just with my mom. Just with my journal, just with God.

There were lots of bike rides. Lots of cows, lots of corn, lots of wheat.

Of course, I *wanted* to talk it out; put a quarter in me, and I'll spew. And part of me wanted so desperately to find a safe place to remember, to do the messy laugh-cry as I sorted through all my hampers, all my laundry, that whole stained tangle of feelings and fears and worries and guilt. But I knew I couldn't do that with my friends. Because if I started, poured my heart out—*all the way out*—I knew I would never be able to put the cap back on. And

I knew it'd sound like opera—all rousing and rich, hot pitch and passion, but wasted on a listener who couldn't possibly begin to grasp the language.

And that's why I never told my best friends about the morning I spent blowing snot into tie after tie. It would just be vibrato to them. I couldn't bring myself to ask them: to just push pause, stop their lives, leave school; to just sit there on my bedroom floor, watching wordlessly, resist the wiggly urge to stand up and fix something.

The truth is: I was never as brave or bold as Job.

Job was a prosperous farmer who lost it all.

Absolutely *everything*.

The story opens almost backstage, a bit of drama happening higher, in the spiritual realm. But those underpinnings aside—since we humans don't get to see them—I want to focus on the story as Job would have undoubtedly told it: from his one-point perspective.

It happened like this. One day, word comes to a very rich Job that raiders have stolen all 500 teams of his oxen and all 500 of his female donkeys; the thieves have slaughtered his farmhands, too.

Before Job can react—literally, while the first messenger is still midsentence—a second messenger bursts in with more news. Lightning—or "fire from heaven"—has struck, burning the sheep—all 7,000 of them—and their shepherds alike.

And wait.

As if that weren't enough, a third messenger topples the other two, and delivers the knockout: Job's sons and daughters had been feasting in the eldest's home, and a surge of wind swept in from the desert, and *thwam!* The place caved like a house of cards, killing the kids in mere minutes.

Every last one.

Job stands up. He tears his robe, shaves his head, falls facedown before God. He prays a prayer so faithful that it had to have physically hurt as he mouthed it. Each word, like he's winding his heart in a vise. He is broken, but not beyond repair, and he speaks the bald truth…something that runs along the lines of "I came in with nothing, and I didn't plan on taking anything out."

That he'll praise God all the same.

And if that is where the story ended, maybe Job would be a bit more celebritized, action-figured, sold to us in Sunday school right alongside the likes of Noah, and Abraham, and Moses. Wasn't Job's the same sort of big trust that bravely and blindly obeys? The same faith required to build arks, bring the impossible offering, cleave waters?

But the story doesn't stop. Not there.

We have part two. Job's health fails; his skin erupts into a case of boils, head-to-toe wounds that he scrapes with a shard of pottery, the bleeding buying but seconds of relief. His wife is more pragmatic: She suggests that Job quit acting so noble and curse God already. But, still itching, he puts her in her place.

Looks at her, square, and says that she's talking like a godless woman. "Shall we accept good from God, and not trouble?"[1]

Bitten by boils, and his faith has not budged.

Job makes me look like a toddler kicking in the grocery cart.

In the freshness of Job's grief, his buddies come, tearing their robes and tossing dirt in the air, "sitting shivah" with him. Squatting on the ground for seven days and nights, not saying a word.

Not a peep, not a "Hey buddy," not an "Are you doing okay?" They knew: His grief was too deep for words.

They were willing to just be near him, to go at his pace, to follow his lead.

They cared.

When Job starts to talk, finally, what falls out first—after a week of rumination and silence and floor-sitting—is that he wishes he'd never been born. What was the point, he says, to be nursed and raised and blessed for *this*?

And with that invitation, the friends wind up. One by one, they submit that Job must have sinned. There has to be some rational reason for the fallout. This has to be some sort of divine bookkeeping, punishment, some settlement for an outstanding debt. Examine your steps, Job, they say. Then repent. Repent, repent, repent.

This goes back and forth; it's downright painful to read. How do you defend your innocence while bearing such sorrow? While hungry, wounds weeping? While your friends are busy making sense of the situation, writing prescriptions for pains they can't possibly feel?

Job says:

With high hopes, the caravans from Tema and from Sheba stop for water, but finding none, their hopes are dashed. You, too, have proved to be of no help. You have seen my calamity, and you are afraid.[2]

But the friends keep shaking salt in the wounds. There's no refreshment, nothing to ice Job's anger, no succor for the sting. They were off to a flawless start with the silent floor-sitting, with their pure presence, but then they opened their mouths and shot arrows.

Good advice at the wrong time can feel more like a club than a scalpel.

I'm thinking this the moment the airplane seat-belt sign blinks off. I lean forward to dig out my carry-on, pull it up from where it's slid beneath the seat in front of me.

I stand to stretch my legs, sling the bag on my shoulder. The aisle floods, a snake of sleepy people who begin unlatching overhead compartments and pulling on wool hats. Cocooning up in their coats. It's March, and I am back in New York, home from an overnight in Chicago. In a way, it almost feels like the trip didn't happen, because it came and went that quickly: Yesterday, I was sitting at work, fuddling with a press release, when my boss came into my office and told me to quit hemming and hawing and just go. *Leave already.* Head straight to the airport or I'd regret it.

Because it's not every day your mother is made a guest of the *Oprah Winfrey Show.*

Mom had seen the query: Oprah's website panning for women who were slightly disgruntled and facing a messy midlife. Mom had just turned fifty and figured she fit the bill: At thirty-nine, she'd lost both parents. At forty-five, her husband. And now, despite returning to college and earning her bachelor's, then master's, in art education, both degrees have turned out to be squibs. She's had exactly zero luck landing a full-time teaching job, despite being wolfish for one.

Despite netting a string of long-term subbing jobs, one right after another.

Despite winning each principal's verbal allegiance.

Somehow, it always stalls. The offers die on the vine.

"They want the spring chickens," she tells me. "They'll choose a funky twenty-something. One with the vampy haircut and a hidden tattoo and no real life experience."

Turning fifty amplifies the emotion, the gloom, so she sits

down and clacks out an e-mail, pitching herself to the show, and why not? She's feeling a little bit lost. And fidgety. And so she says it: *Midlife crisis is a real thing.*

She leans back and rereads what she's written. Then figures she'd better let the e-mail cool a half hour while she fixes a salad for dinner. After she's eaten, stacked her bowl in the sink, she sits back down at the computer. She sighs, she shrugs, and hits Send. And she doesn't expect what comes next.

The video team arrives at the house. They need B-roll: something to cue up her story. The producer asks Mom if she has any old movies, something from when the kids were growing up, and Mom nods, goes right to the closet and pulls a cardboard box down from the high shelf. Rifles through. There: a good one, Christmas 1992. The year we waltzed like sugarplum fairies in the family room and almost knocked down the tree.

Mom is nostalgic, loves honoring history; she is kind to her memories, loves dusting them off and keeping them clean and sometimes playing them back. That's why, when she pops the cassette in the player and sits down on the couch, the inevitable happens: She reaches for a throw pillow, pulls it tight like a teddy, and the tiny tributaries begin their flow down her cheeks, along the ledge of her nose.

As she brushes them off with her thumb, the camera leans in.

We land in Chicago. Me, my cousin, my two aunts, because we're Mom's paparazzi, entourage; we're big dusty moths swirling all around in her light. It's not quite spring, and the city stretches out cold, endless cement and glitter and glamour, a Magnificent Mile of twinkling shops and lumbering limos. It is Gucci, Louis

Vuitton, Burberry. Ralph Lauren. Jo Malone perfume. Everything looks clean and chic and electric—*caffeinated*—and there's
no sticking snow, and the tingling begins as we start trading
what-ifs, imagining what miracles await my mother.

Maybe there'll be a makeover? At least a little one? Maybe
she'll be surprised backstage with a fresh blend of highlights and
lowlights and a revelatory jawline haircut…maybe even a mod
little scarf? Something punchy to wear to her next job interview?
A pair of $200 Louboutin pumps for her Payless closet?

We share the limo with another guest—a woman in a baby-blue
blazer and natty glasses. We all smile, say hello, squeeze in. All
seven of us. The woman is classy, confident, glossy-haired. She's
just there with her plus-one, her beau, but we are legion. There are
five of us, including Mom; it's like she's brought her whole wireless network.

The limo pulls out into traffic, and we ask the woman why she
wrote in.

She's eschewed a finance career, she says. She is now living a
new life crafting artisanal chocolates.

We lean a little closer as the story unfolds, and it is intoxicating
and impossible: It is epiphanic. She uses habaneros in her ganache.
The way she tells it, it is wild and wonderful and widens the sky;
it smells like possibility and thumps like a good film, drumming
hard and heavy in your chest as you walk out of the theater.

After we've properly salivated at the romance of her new life as
a confectioner, she does the polite thing and reciprocates, asking
Mom for her story.

Mom tells me later that this is the moment her palms start to
sweat.

"I think," she says, "I am the project."

★　　★　　★

My mom sits in a front row, in full view of the camera, and we settle in for a good look at Oprah, here in the flesh, all polished in a shiny taupe blouse that peeks perfectly from a deep V-neck sweater. Her hair is in a low-slung, loose pony, a bouquet of curls. She is wearing peach earrings and a look of authority.

My mom has chosen a periwinkle top that sets her blue eyes fierce, and a pair of pants a smidge tight—they split in the dressing room earlier, an honest-to-goodness wardrobe malfunction. No worries; someone on crew brought back safety pins before the makeup artist finished dabbing a steely cream shadow just inside Mom's lash line. Sitting now, legs crossed at the ankles, she looks beautiful and broken.

The show gets rolling, and my mom's palms prove themselves right: Other guests have arrived in other limos, each packing so much chutzpah she could be a 5-hour energy drink. Each is uncommonly wonderful, having moved from success to success like she was shifting bars on a trapeze: from university dean to touring musician; from lawyer to martial arts master; from talk show host to self-employed florist.

And, of course: from Wall Street to Willy Wonka.

When it's time for my mother to follow these gale-force women who went from great to greater, her package runs, and there she is: a woman who can't find her way off the sofa.

They try to help Mom a little. Give her a public pep talk. The real guest star of today's episode is a spiritual coach, a willowy woman in a daring skirt, with bony and beautifully articulated kneecaps. She's written a book and is probably pinned up with a mic, maybe threaded up the back of her blouse. I work in PR now, so I know what this means: She is here as the expert. And she is thereby compelled to spend a good bit of time presuming to know.

To implicitly understand.

She tries. She tries to cheerlead, honestly; to rah–rah; to speak hope and fan something bright in Mom's belly.

If you make the brave move and unfurl your wings, you'll fly, she assures.

Oprah echoes a version of this. She tells the audience how *we think our way into our realities,* and she is firm about it. *If you open yourself to good things, they* will *find their way in.*

Lots of this, this flying and unfurling and spreading open. They wave the words like they're magic wands: *Alignment. Energy. Emerge.*

And my mom sits still like a schoolgirl, lips pursed and legs tight; only I can tell she's about ready to burst. And when she can't possibly sit quiet any longer, she says it.

But I have spread my wings.

Because she's taken some big-girl steps to reimagine herself, to restart, to engineer her own midlife miracle: She's gotten remarried and become a grandmother; she's funded her dream and gone back to school. She's tried to move the metaphorical mountains with her mind.

But what if, sometimes, even all that isn't enough?

When we leave, the guests get a free box of chocolates and the teacher's latest book. The candy's inspired, sure, but as I thumb through the hardcover on the flight home, fanning the air up from its pages and trying so hard to breathe in its balm, I can't help but close my eyes and shake my head at how even the most earnest advice can actually hurt.

How good intentions can sometimes sting.

How, in twenty-four hours, you *can* take to wing, and fly, and unfurl, and yet arrive right back where you started: on the same stretch of cement, more un-understood than you felt in the first place.

I take a bite of a chocolate, and it helps a little.

Job survives, but there's more to sweat through first. After questioning the so-called comforts of his moralizing pals, he moves on to bigger things.

Like questioning God.

"I cry to you, O God, but you don't answer me. I stand before you, and you don't bother to look."[3]

The friends hear Job's irreverent words, all this tongue aimed smack at God, and they reprise. Attack anew. They tell Job he is arrogant; they tell him God is *just*. That God is powerful, that God pays attention.

It's an angry, seething spiral; finger-pointing, finger-wagging. Friends trying to fix, but only making a mess, because honestly: How could they have answers to things so far above their pay grade?

Because, really: Who fields the hardest questions?

In the final chapters, God comes to Job in the whirlwind. He begins his slow answer back...an answer, supposedly, but it looks a whole lot more like a question.

See, God doesn't pull up a PowerPoint, doesn't thumb through his blueprints, doesn't bring Job in on some grand cosmological secret. And he doesn't offer to make sense of Job's mayhem. What he does do is this: He asks for an alibi.

He issues the world's longest rhetorical question, one that simply asks Job *where he was*.

Where was he, when God was measuring the universe, the planets still cold in his palms?

When God was manning storehouses of snow, telling oceans just how far they might lick, lap, and flow?

When he was pluming the ostrich? Pinning feathers on the stork? Teaching the hawk to hunt and hover, feast and fly?

Job reads between the lines, and shrinks down small. Smaller. He realizes he's not even close to being able to approach the bench, to cross-question God about why he does what he does. Why he allows hard hurts to happen.

In his own way, Job hears what God means, but never quite says: "My answers are bigger than your questions, Job. Your job isn't to know, but to trust that I do."

I don't think it's wrong to kick and scream, to claim you're confused, to stuff questions in the comment box, to shake clenched fists at heaven. I have. Lots. It's actually a move in the right direction; it's the sort of searching, seeking, knocking that Jesus calls holy art.

Maybe the risk comes when we *silence* the doubt; when we stifle it, try to pet it down, confusing real comfort with our need for firm answers. Pave a world with stock answers and rosy, good guesses, and the greatest fact gets ignored: that we humans will only ever know part of the story. That our vision is limited, that we drive with blind spots.

That we are not God.

But to those of us who can yield to the mystery—who can bend low, curling into the same posture as Job—God gives us rest. We who come bone-weary, who relent to humbly know that God knows: We find peace. Peace is always ultimately about posture; about admitting that we're small. The river-kind of peace that flows and fills the thirsty? It bubbles up from the big knowledge that God's mind isn't our mind; that his ways aren't ours either. That he has the higher clearance, entrée to whole archives and databases, a full intelligence we do not.

Peace comes when we finally, often even reluctantly, nod and decide to agree: that his is a perfect knowing.

That he knows.

Chapter Nine

ONE MORE JUMP

There is a sacredness in tears. They are not the mark of weakness, but of power. They speak more eloquently than ten thousand tongues. They are messengers of overwhelming grief . . . and unspeakable love.
—Washington Irving, nineteenth-century American writer

I don't visit Dad's grave. I try, though. I drive within a mile of the cemetery and then turn around. Get a drive-thru coffee. Turning right, pulling through the iron gate, it feels too committal. Too official. I need to do it all alone, but coming near feels like approaching a black hole, suicidal, like I'm asking to be sucked up, vacuumed in.

It feels unnecessary, too, when there are so many other places I can summon him.

One fail-safe place is the infield of my high school's track—a shabby old runway once leading to the pole-vault pit. There is a spot of grass that's watered with my sweat, and a place where Dad and I planted our only shared dream: for sports fame, school records, and most important, my clearing a ten-foot crossbar.

Three years that dream kicked hard and strong. Then, on a sticky summer night, it died.

Dad followed close behind.

Finally reaching the runway, I collapse beside it, on the lawn. The sun is licking up the dew; it's bound to be a gorgeous day.

Squatting down, I pull the zipper of my duffel and begin digging through the main compartment.

"What have you eaten this morning?" Dad asks. He's a self-proclaimed sports nutritionist on meet days.

I squint, raising my hand in front to block the June rays. "So far, cereal. But I'm planning on more."

His hand slides into a frayed pocket, finds the leather wallet, flips it open. He tugs at Lincoln. Handing it over, he tips his head to the booster tent: It's still brunch time, but already, I see volunteers scraping grills, stacking big bags of buns, boxes of frozen burgers.

"Okay, in a little bit. I'll just have some of my energy shake for now."

He nods. "Got your spikes? You're gonna be real fast plowing down that runway."

I bite my tongue, reach for patience, just nod. I'm hoping he'll catch the hint that I need some time to regroup, to get in the zone. Everywhere, athletes are warming up; butt kickers, high knees, Smurf-skips, lunges, quick feet. Nervous and antsy, they spring, spastic as jumping beans. Shaking a leg like you de-crumb a tablecloth. Webbing and turning their hands inside out in a stretch, yoga salutes to the sun.

Reaching, bending, always moving.

Most parents have staked out a row of bleachers, but Dad stands right here, beside the runway, upturns a green sack and jiggles it until something slides out. Pressing the center, a heap of canvas explodes into a camp chair. He smiles at me, points again to the concession tent, and waves.

He saunters off.

I'm finally alone, and I get down to work. I lift the clean, white laces of my featherweight slippers, and they spin, twirl, dangle, so light they almost float. I smile.

Coach Wood swears there's magic in new shoes.

Dad and I have made a special trip for these, down to a small, steep-priced sports specialty store tucked into a dicey wedge of the city. He cringed, a little—tried to mask it, but I saw—as he pushed the bills down onto the counter, slowly but nobly, as if he knew it was necessary. I cradled the box on my lap the whole way home, open, turning the shoes over in my hands, counting the spikes that came in the little plastic bag, making sure I had one to screw into each hole.

This morning, I take the wrench, give each spike a final, snug twist, and my new shoes have teeth. Incisors. They'll claw the ground and help me run. I set them aside so I can take a couple of loops around the track in my old sneaks, and the jog pulls my muscles into warm taffy.

When Dad comes back, he's chewing, halfway through a burger. For as long as I can remember, he's been pushing this, my jumping. Sillicks have natural spring, he says. My grandfather, his dad, medaled Illinois state champ in the long jump and was invited to the Olympic trials. He wound up missing them after pulling a groin muscle, not that it would have changed much: Those would have been the 1936 Games in Berlin, the summer Jesse Owens ascended to power, sweeping four golds and outshining the sun. Still, Grandpa's legend hung over me, dangling like a dare, and when no one was watching I'd slip out to the back door and lay out a stray stick, or the shaft of a rake, and then back up to give myself plenty of airstrip. This running and bounding was a game, mostly, but I also was itching my curiosity just the littlest bit, in case I'd inherited anything.

I hadn't.

Still, Dad kept sowing seeds: I should try vaulting, he said. He nailed a chin-up bar from the rafters in the garage, and I'd jump up to grab it, see how many I could eke out. And then one cold spring morning, on a whim, I did it; I showed up to varsity track tryouts in a pair of squeaky high-tops—my eighth-grade basketball shoes, left over from an earlier failed sports debut.

I told the coaches I was a jumper, not a runner. I was trying out for *field*. They took my name down on their clipboard, shrugged, and handed me a stick. It was the first year that girls could compete, and they needed someone to try it. And there I was, hand up, waving.

We didn't jump right away; we snapped those bars over and over, a *slam-slam-slam* against the hard gym floor, counting paces, learning the dance: when to lift the knee, how to hold the arms stiff and straight, bicep smushed up next to your nose when you plant the pole.

And then we went outside, and jumped.

And I guess I did it pretty well.

Leaning forward in his chair, Dad pops a final bite of meat into his mouth, sucks a bit of mustard off his fingertips.

"You'd better stay cool," he says. "Heat will suck you like an orange."

I duck into the shade of his chair and shut my eyes. The boys are still competing, taking longer than expected; at this rate, I've got a few hours before I have to rev up for real. I have to clear my mind, relax. Think of nothing. But I can't.

This is my last season, and if I place here today, there are trophies.

State qualifying meets.

Dreams.

I stand up again, then sit down again, then mosey over to a few friends; I find ways to distract myself for the better part of the afternoon.

"You should probably think about warming up again," Dad says. "Here comes a bunch of hors d'oeuvres."

I survey the field. Dad's right. A flock of thin-armed newbies has gathered on the sidelines, poles limp in their hands. They look like little wet olives, hugging toothpicks, and I smirk at how perfect it is, our code name for them. Dwarfed by their sticks, they're tentative, goofy, a sort of pregame show. *Hors d'oeuvres.* The appetizers. The lucky ones will clear opening height, which, at five feet, is lower than what the high-jumper medalists will manage— no pole included.

I look at those girls, watching closer. I don't remember that timidity.

Almost from the get-go—in spite of taking off on the wrong foot every time—I muscled my way over enough crossbars to be handed the blue ribbons that proclaimed me Freshman and Junior Varsity County Champion. My dad politely ignored the fact that my technique was uglier than sin. "Hey, a clear's a clear," he'd say with a grin, cheering as wildly as if it were Monday Night Football. I loved every minute of him loving it.

Loving me.

The boys are nearing the end of their contest. Only one is left, a flaxen-haired one. He's pasty-skinned with a pair of duck lips, big pink ones that never quite smile. He's already won, technically, but he's got three jumps remaining, so he drags his fiberglass pole back onto the red runway. The stick's eleven feet long and an inch in diameter, but he wields it like a majorette would a baton. Afternoons of practice have turned it into an extension of his body.

A whisper befalls the small crowd that's amassed. This is Tommy Barker. Sucking in a deep breath, those fat candy lips turn farther down, a frown of concentration. He pretends he doesn't see this audience, but he knows we're here, and he's imbibing. His calloused hands search the pole for the worn tape that marks his grip, and he squeezes it, extends his arms, stretches his calves, and mock-sprints in place. He counts the paces of his run out under his breath, closes his eyes, pictures success. I know, because I do it, too, the imagery. I close my own eyes and feel the rush of a swift run, firm takeoff, strong press. A liquid inversion, clean clear, and flyaway.

You rehearse this now, because the moment your legs start to pump—*one, two, three, four*—and you fire up a run—*five, six, seven, eight*—there will be no time for details of thought. The mind signs over responsibility to the body; you switch to autopilot, a sort of competition cruise control. If he engages his brain, he'll wrench it—"paralysis by analysis," Coach says. So you center. You go blank, you barrel down, you fling yourself skyward and trust your training and instinct and pray the dream to materialize.

Barker knows this.

And here he goes. Dad and I watch, loving and hating him all at once as he gathers his bulk, stacks his vertebrae as high as he can till he's up on his toes. Frozen still, he pauses, cocked and ready, not even breathing. We hold this last lungful, too.

Then it collapses, this tower that is his body, and he guns down the runway, fast and fluid, the tip of his pole falling steadily with each step.

He's up high, and it's so close, as he so barely grazes the bar.

But it's enough to send it into free fall. Two times more we watch, the whole procession, until he's officially out. There's respectful applauding anyway, a golf clap for his courage, his noble finish. I put my hands together, even though I always found this part odd: Even coming in first, the unrelenting vaulter ends on a miss.

Gymnastic, technical, nonperfectible—that's the vault.

The standards are lowered, the crossbar removed, and like buzzards we girls move in, lining up for a turn to check our stride, backward from the pit, to measure our steps out, mark them with tape. One girl wears a helmet, a long, chestnut ponytail poking out the back. Almost equestrian. There are about forty pairs of tanned, toned arms whapping poles down in position, flexing on tiptoe, their arms thrusting up and out the split second their poles smack the ground. Each waits her turn to test a run.

By the pit, in no big hurry, Leslie Moore slips off her sunglasses and snap-side track pants. And I sigh. She's practically professional. Her trainer, face obscure and shapeless beneath the brim of his sun hat, rubs his chin stubble as they discuss her handhold. Businesslike, and she's in high school. He plucks the cap off a large, cylindrical tube, like a giant can of Pick-Up Sticks, an armamentarium of hundred-plus-dollar poles, and draws out two. She nods, chin pointing to the one in his left hand. *That's* the one.

I stare at my slim, smooth stick, and whisper to it.

You and me.

Moore steps onto the runway, and the last girl scurries off the mat. Everything is textbook; Moore drives hard, full throttle, deliberate and graceful, the pole sliding neatly into the metal box as she peaks tall, a ballerina. She presses forward, arms sturdy, unmoving, and her body bends into a backward C. The pole pulls her up, she rides skyward, rolling and rowing, heels to heaven, and she's flying.

She rolls off the mat, dismayed.

Her trainer says her turn was too late, and she puppy-dog nods.

The horseback girl, the one in the helmet, is next. She looks over her shoulder, swallows hard, as if to make sure that it's really her run.

It is. Her gallops are goofy, sprint loose and jerky, a wild Black Beauty, and I am reminded that this is not as easy as Moore makes it look. You can bang out a jump in mere seconds, sure, but it's a dozen tiny moves spliced together.

Each must be perfect.

We find our marks and check in. I know there will be no real competition today; Moore will win, a foot above the rest, and we know it.

And that's fine. Today, Dad and I are not vying to beat her. We've joked about it, sure, but we both laid it to rest a while ago. It's our last meet, and there's a more private laurel we're chasing.

"Today's the day." Dad stands up and pretends he's holding a stick, emphatically punching his arms out and locking them. He grunts. "But you're going to have to press, and hard."

I nod. I have to attack, force my pole to arc. It's the only way I'll load it with enough energy to clear ten feet.

I warm up some more as the competition begins. I wait out a few rounds for the bar to be raised. I don't want to waste my energy on the baby jumps I know I can clear.

Finally, it's at eight feet. Time to start.

"Turner up, Mark on deck, Sillick in the hole."

It's been a long day, and the sun is now beneath the tree line, starting to throw the first shadows. Most other events have medaled already, most moms and dads and sisters and brothers have filtered out from the stands. The empty bleachers must have that evening chill to them, lonely for beating sun and warm bodies, and the track is quiet, the finish line fallen asleep, as the field lights flicker, hesitant, then resolve to beam. Everything seems concrete, illuminated. Dad yawns, and I pretend I do not see; he's late for a campout at my uncle's creek, but he won't budge till we're done and I know it. We have dreamed of this night. We have waited all day.

We have waited years.

The vault drags on.

"Sillick up." The key is impatient. The official stares at her stopwatch, makes sure I am taking position. I yank my warm-ups off over my flats; they snag on the spikes, and I pull harder. Goose bumps prickle up, and I run a hand over my calves, shooing them away.

I close my eyes. I can do this.

And I lift, air in, and I pray, air out, and then I'm speeding down, slicing dusk, smooth along the lit pathway, and I ram my arms forward, trying to hold them out strong. But the day of waiting, the sun, has suckled them weak like Dad warned. I take off at the box, and the pole starts to lift, but I'm slow and I know it's too little and I start to sputter midair. So I hold on, keep clinging, trying to plan my next move—then I'm coming down backward, the same way I came, pole loading, loading, until I let go, and it flings up and out, *thwam*, clips my bicep and almost spears an official.

That was bad, I think, but I shake it off; I keep walking. I rub my arm, a bluish bruise blooming beneath my skin. It's ugly under these brash bulbs.

Dad and Coach lean nearer, both with knit brows, and I mouth "I'm fine," waving them back. But it's not fine. It kills.

When you jump, you have to walk onto the runway clear-headed. *Every time.* You need to forget the last miss, forgive mistakes, sometimes in the matter of a minute. It's the only way to rally confidence to plow down a strip of cement and fling yourself ten feet up.

I make my mind an Etch-a-Sketch; I shake the picture out.

That never happened.

Except that it *did*. And when they call my name, and I line up again, and I run, I know there's no fight left. The throbbing of my arm throws the rhythm of my stride, and without a clean takeoff, I have nothing.

I miss a second time, walk over to Dad. He squeezes my shoulders in encouragement, not willing to jinx me with advice.

Alone at the end of the runway, I huff out a prayer. Close my eyes. *Run.* And that third time, when the bar falls, I lie there a moment; I look up at the night sky, too new for stars, and I do not want to get up from the mat.

I am out.

We walk back to the van and drive home. The pole hangs awkwardly out my window, cutting between us, and the wind is lapping into the cabin, and something is swelling in the throat. I have been turning over the idea of college meets in my head, as some sort of consolation; I look over to Dad, his hand on the wheel as he stares forward, and I want so badly to pipe up and be brave, to bandy about how maybe there will be another meet, another chance, but there won't. We both know it. So we just sit there, watching the yellow dashes, the seam of the road, wind gusty and cold like we're sailing, crushing waves. I pet down my hair. And I try to keep swallowing, to not choke on this dead dream, and the emptiness actually aches.

Two months later, he is gone.

That fall, in search, I pedal my bike past the dusty construction zone two miles from my house. My high school is installing an all-weather track that boasts to be among the finest in western New York.

But I bypass this brand-new project, the spongy turf a frivolity I'll never know, and keep going till I find myself back on the old vault runway.

The asphalt here is cracked in at least four places, and grass has crept up over the sides. There are no metal standards shouldering a crossbar, just cerulean sky, and a mound of upturned soil is all that remains of the box where I used to plant the pole. The box has recently been dug up and stored away in a shed somewhere, or moved to the new track completely. Or heavens, *thrown out.* Where the mat once rested is a brown, balding bit of earth, a square where the sun could never shine.

The runway dead-ends, a stretch of stone leading nowhere, and I feel it, the deep empty of this clean-swept field.

And I realize, then, what's missing most: the man who I now know loved vaulting more than I did.

I know that, for the rest of my life, whenever I drive past that old, abandoned track, I'll squint. I'll be looking for those two pieces of tape that showed my start, and I'll imagine fussing over them, pulling the mark back, forth, and back again, wondering why my step was off, trying to be consistent, trying to nail it, asking Dad to watch closer and figure out where I was reaching, or chopping, or if I was crashing my arms rather than pushing them out stick-straight.

I will see him, armed with a Butterfinger and blue Gatorade, ready to refuel me and chant the superstitious phrases that make sense only to us. He'll set everything down on the ground, take his post at the box, eager to be my eyes, to obsess with me, *C'mon, let's do this.*

He will be there.

And, just on cue, halfway down my neck there'll be a knot, a little half hitch, the kind that makes me smile and cry and love him and miss him and feel him, all at once, and my body will switch into some gear where it rides funny, some gear it was not made for, and I become a bit of a mess, the lonely, little-girl version of myself, wishing she could be tall enough, strong enough, to reach heaven and yank him down, just one more jump.

It is not just this runway that leads me to him; too many things are Dad, so soaked in his scent. It was just as Mom has said: *He has divided.* Every holiday, tradition, put into before and after baskets; memories made and yet-to-be-made suddenly tagged by this new timeline; new rituals, new rules. For a while, it was *crash, bump, smack,* into the very furniture of my life.

Literally: his chair at the kitchen table, his dresser, his treadmill, the little man-cave bar he'd built in the basement. His tool bench, a clutter of old radios and dead flashlights and big Folgers cans collecting nails and screws. These everywhere reminders, death's debris, inspired many a twinge—each demanding that I wash it away, loosen its grip with a fury of tears. And I did. I wept hard in those moments, because those cries were proof: Dad had scooped me out, right from my middle; spooned out a big pit, like I was a melon. I had the hole, hollowed here, and I still needed his love to fill it.

Dad's older brother died just a year after he did. My uncle was a writer, a thinker, a woodworking philosopher with calloused hands. Honest eyes. A wry grin. He was an English teacher, a columnist, a farmer; he planted strawberries, and milked cows, and sugared maples. He planted ideas, though, mostly; he posed the big questions, his prose earthy, and playful, and lyrical. He could write about a handful of loam like it was caviar; he'd pat a pocket of beans like they were gold doubloons.

The man saw the world for the wonder it was.

And then, almost a year to the day Dad died, my uncle fell from his tractor. He'd been moving logs on his property, and he backed up just a bit too far, into an old barn's foundation. The tractor, as if running by ghost, continued to circle, running him over.

My aunt found him, and the injuries were profound—a ruptured esophagus, collapsed lung. He was airlifted to the emergency department, admitted to the ICU, and frantic phone calls and e-mails ensued. I was away at school by then, my sophomore year. I kept close tabs on the updates, scanning for prognoses, vitals, and folding my prayers accordingly until messages started filtering in further and further apart, and it seemed like maybe things were becoming stable, like he was going to climb out.

But one day, the winds shifted. And he was gone.

I am shut in my dorm room one snowy night, only months later, when his daughter—my cousin—calls me on the phone.

She's carried his torch into the classroom; she's a teacher, too. She's a little bit older than I am, and she and I don't talk often enough; Dad grew up one of seven, and I have cousins by the carful.

My sophomore year roommate, fortunately, has brought a wireless phone that gets pretty good range, so I take it into the dorm bathroom across the hall. My cousin and I say hello, bush-beat a little, but it doesn't take long to get past pleasantries, and she makes her confession: The tears almost feel good.

Too good.

It's like they bring him back, she says, and she is scared to ever stop crying them.

The bathroom is a bit of a funhouse, with mirrors and counters ringing almost all the way around, and that night, watching myself on the phone from too many angles, I realize: Maybe growing up is, in one part, measured by our capacity to not wince when we see our reflection in other people.

I am finding myself all too easily in her words.

I nod as she tries to explain it, and I wish the phone would register all my head bobbing. All the up and down, "I know, uh-huh," over and over, an oversung chorus.

I tell her about the track. The infield, how I ride there. Stand there. Wish.

How I like to be alone with him.

She gets it.

The tears are good at repelling, I say, at keeping the commoners out, roping off all the upturned parts of the heart. The rubble we don't want others to see.

And, maybe, yeah, the tears are part magic, too. They beckon; a good cry, and Dad is *back*. I don't know how or why it works either, I say. Maybe they moisten and unstiffen grief; they smooth things over, and a hard cry can even feel *good*.

Almost like a hug, yes.

And yet.

I wanted to tell her, but didn't know if it was too soon. I was fifteen months along in life without Dad, and already, I could tell. Something was happening, if in a small, quiet way, like the first not-yet-fragrant, not-yet-unfurled blossoms needling their way to the edge of the arms of a tree. I didn't understand it, couldn't see it, but I sensed it. Something, some part of Dad, was still alive—and not just when channeled through tears.

I just didn't know how to say it, not yet.

We hung up, and I wished I could hug her.

If I had been braver that night on the phone, I might have admitted that, already, my grief was changing. That every so often, I'd feel the tears steeping, but then they'd be shunted by a sudden smile, a giggle. I should have said that. Sure, they still came, startled me, their taps on the shoulder in the most unholy places, but maybe...maybe they didn't always dig their nails in quite so deep. They didn't always break skin. I was able to slowly, sometimes, on lucky occasion, access a memory that starred Dad without having to pay such an exorbitant up-front fee; the home videos still registered a dull drumming ache, but not the hard gasping cries they had initially.

Maybe I should have said that it would get a little bit better.

Therapeutic on so many levels, I think tears don't get enough good press. But they deserve it; they're workhorses, smoothing out the curved surface, always rounding the eye so we can see. They're antimicrobial, too, teeming with secretions that disarm bacteria, and—while we don't pay them much notice until they pool and fall—those tears are infinite. Always there. Always busy, hosing off hurtful agents: the speck of dust, the wayward bug, the sweat of onions. We blink, and the tears do their work, shielding sensitive tissues beneath.

During the big cries—when they do much more than lube, but actually burble out, little rivulets right down your cheeks—those tears also rid stress chemicals, flushing toxins that would otherwise collect in your body.

Tears, then, work hard on multiple fronts: They're built-in eye-gear, an emotional weather vane, and, quite simply, just another excretory organ.

In a way, tears and pearls aren't a far cry apart. Pearls form along similar lines; they're also the fruit of a body desperately trying to shoo something out. An irritant—a piece of sand, a parasite, a teeny-tiny crab or fish—slips into the oyster's flesh, its mantle. Almost instantly, the immune function revs, and the mantle starts churning out nacre, coating the irritant in a series of platelets.

It's a miniature masonry, really, almost like building with brick and spreading mortar, and the pearl is glued together layer by layer, each one so whisper-thin it mirrors the wavelength of visible light. This kind of, well, *crying*, is fine, fussy work—it can take an oyster years to turn out a pearl just the size of a pea.

Is it worth it? The tough, lustrous gem, seeded deep in the flesh? The pain turned precious, hidden within? I don't know. What I do know, when I crack the shell, hold it high, see the way sun dances on surface, a milky, muted glow ... what I know is that sometimes it reflects a rainbow so stunning that I hardly remember it began as an ache.

I am not the first to suggest that there's meaning in this miracle, and I won't be the last. But those first jabs, those first crashes after

Dad died... they felt very much like nuisances, and, just a little, I feel for the oyster.

I didn't like my invaders much either; not the way they scraped at my most vulnerable parts, not their timing, always so inconvenient. Their sting always demanded answers on my part, and so I kept washing them, bit by bit—my feeble tries at fencing them off.

But something, now, was happening. *It was.* Daily, in little ways, I was beginning to see: Sometimes, I was no longer smashing into the memories so much as I was happening upon them. Dad's music on an audiotape, on a good day, might evoke a careful smile; a curly-haired stranger with heaps of freckles could be his twin, and for a moment, there it was: the flutter of remembrance.

A twinge, but yet, I could breathe.

The tears were doing tedious work, so much more than I'd ever know, and the healing had started, imperceptibly. It was happening, layer by layer.

This—maybe this is what I should have told my cousin.

Chapter Ten

LAWNMOWER MAN

See, I am doing a new thing!
Now it springs up; do you not perceive it?
I am making a way in the wilderness
and streams in the wasteland.

—Isaiah 43:19

I am standing on the stoop of our garage, watching my mom bend over the mower. She clicks a lever into the start position, gives a yank, rowing like it's Olympic sport.

Nothing.

She bends again, gives another haul. Another.

She rechecks the lever's position—no, that's right—and puts her hands to her head, trying to remember if there is a step she's missed.

Enough gas, okay.

Oiled—she pumps the little black ball a few times to prime it.

And then just tug like heck and pray the sucker howls to life, right? Isn't that how this thing works?

Three more rows, and there's not so much as the thrill of a false start. Mom looks at the mower, not sure which one of them is broken, and curses it.

"Pat," she heaves, "you knew you were dying! Why didn't you show me how?"

To my dad's discredit, his make-believe games of "I'm not sick" did little to prepare us for life without him.

There were many lawnmower moments where we wished he'd taken a minute to let us imagine, if only so that we could cut the grass without breaking down, doubled over, feeling lost on so many levels.

Now, as I write this, thirty-one years old and married, my husband and I have already taken out term life insurance, our bad bets on each other. We've had the policies forever, practically since we got out of college. The monthly payment runs about as much as a couple of cheese pizzas, and believe me, the peace of mind tastes better.

My mother's story gets better, though.

So much so, in fact, that I hesitate sharing this next part, because it seems such a sharp deviation from reality, better suited to film, where you expect these ironies to thicken the plot—cinematic corn starch, if you will. But no, this story's true. And maybe I need to mark this chapter with an asterisk, tuck in a fine-print disclaimer stating that the results seen here are not typical.

What God did next for my mother and her broken mower: He let her fall headfirst in love with a small-engine mechanic.

He rebuilds lawn mowers.

His name is Mike.

To know Mike, you might start by visiting his shop. Since he's self-employed, fixing snowblowers, push mowers, riders, the shop is where he coops up most of the day, powered by an enormous mug of coffee, just a pinch of honey, the whine of an old radio. When you walk in, there's a sign nailed to a rafter, running like a banner over everything. It gets right to the point: His services are dependably GOOD, QUICK, and CHEAP, but you can pick only two of the three.

The shop's a small, swirling universe of hardware—O-rings and cotter pins and washers, all meticulously sorted by size into tiny plastic drawers. Drive belts hang off pegs on the walls, various lengths, and there's the cluck and hiss of an air compressor, plastic bottles of all grades of motor oil, a hydraulic lift to the right, and a smart stack of dog-eared supply catalogs, phone book–thick, by the bench. And of course there is Mike, the medic: chestnut hair slicked back, bent over the belly of something broken, a bit of grease smeared just south of one elbow.

Just outside the building, to the left, lies a lawn machine grave-yard, but don't make the mistake of calling those rusty rigs junk. *Junk* is for junkyards. These are *donors*. Though they no longer work independently, Mike knows there is some kind of prom-ise in each: secret, viable parts that can be extracted, dignified, spared from decay and put back to work.

And back to life.

Rebuilding, Mike has taught me, means refusing to write off losses in full. It's about opening your mind to new prospects. It's about mining for good parts and retooling them into something that once again works.

Mike can pick up someone else's "roadkill" off the curb, pro-vide a swift diagnosis, a couple of hours of love, two sweeps of spray paint, and, thanks to Craigslist, give it a new home in some-one's garage. He's salvaged storm-snapped pines in his backyard, too, planing the trunks into the baseboard molding that now runs all around his living room. And then? He grabbed a broom from the closet and swept those wood shavings up from his basement floor.

Then he bagged and sold them as rabbit bedding.

Want one more? A few summers back, my husband helped Mike rescue an old trolling motor that sat at the base of our little lake, maybe had been down there for years. Mike found an old run of rebar, bent it into a hook, and wrestled the engine up like a carp. He let it dry out till it purred soft and pretty.

Somehow, it's like Mike gets a glimpse the rest of us don't; like he sees life four steps out, sniffing potential like only an expert can. He surveys his galaxy of nuts, bolts, belts, and takes a chance on engines others have given up on. Most often, his wager is right.

Of course, he brushes it off when I tell him that this—*this*—is the greatest way he echoes his Maker. Mike, in faith, invests in pieces so seemingly, laughably, beyond hope. He trusts blindly, just believes, and that, as much as I can gather, is the linchpin whenever God wants to do business with (and through) people.

A mammoth ark, in a world that's never tasted rain? New life, taking root in a belly that's barren, old? Let alone in a virgin, never touched?

These may have seemed prime opportunities to politely ask God if you'd heard him right, if he was kidding. If it was possible.

Mike would fight me on this, but he is one of the most faithful people I know.

Mom and Mike met online. Given that *You've Got Mail* is my all-time favorite movie, it might seem that this was all going to be a real kick for me, and it was—only in the stomach. It wasn't that I didn't like Mike, but only that Mike came too fast, about three acts too soon.

But time is a social construct, they say. I suppose that means timing is relative.

Fact is, Mom was pretty lonely after Dad died, hungry for adult company, conversation. And in her mid-forties, with three little women and a busy calendar, that companionship was proving hard to find. It wasn't that having us girls around wasn't enough, she said. But the term "widow" felt wrinkly, and old. Too old. Half her life still stretched on ahead, and she missed having a partner, a sounding board, someone to come home to. Someone to remind her she was precious, desirable—a woman.

It was not until I was married that I fully understood what *that* meant.

This is the era of e-romance, and Mike gets credit for doing that reminding and writing her that first note. The message sat in Mom's queue until late one night, when she finally mustered her courage and volleyed back.

Hello.

Only the next morning, she regretted the decision, thought it a move made too soon. Her fingers swept over the keys, apologetic. She thanked him for his kind words, his overture, but admitted that she was having second thoughts about being ready to "go out there" again. It had been a moment of weakness for her; a false flicker of hope, a trick of the light. Her heart was still bruised, too sore to offer whole.

He understood, and said if she ever was ready, or even just wanted a friendly conversation, to please just let him know.

She wrote back, thanking him for understanding, for not pushing.

He wrote back, telling her that she was welcome.

And then, here is where all the trouble started: Mom wrote

back one more time, thanking Mike for telling her that she was welcome.

In a matter of weeks, the electronic pen pals made the leap to the phone, to the coffee shop, and soon, to each other's homes. We cornered Mom, sat her down at the table, family meeting. We warned her that this was all happening too fast. But she had already floated so far down the river. She was somewhere else. There were three-hour calls where she snuck down to the basement rec room, sat at Dad's bar, giddy as a schoolgirl, legs dangling down the stool, twisting the coiled phone cord around her finger; I know, because that's what she does when she's happy. And because, also, the next morning, I found a lukewarm glass of Diet Coke and a napkin all inked with nervous doodles, the art of someone hoping.

She told us that when you fall in love the second time, it happens much faster than the first; you don't want to wait for your life to start over again. You know what you're missing; you know what you need. You get out the ladder, climb up, and grab it.

I wanted to believe it, but knew I was a poor judge.

I'd not yet fallen in love once.

Somewhere along the way, Mike fixed the mower. He fixed it, then took a Sharpie marker and, like that Grove City T-shirt, he did graffiti; he scribbled its instructions all over it. An annotated lawn mower for the new women in his world: *1. Lift Cap & Check Oil. 2. Press Pump x3 . . .*

And, little by little, we warmed to him, with his muddy boots, and his bear hugs, and his bacon-wrapped meat loaf that looks like a gift. Somehow, these things worked a minor miracle, making us feel a little like a man had come back into our home.

Only, unfortunately—also just like in the movies—it didn't happen quite that smoothly.

The ugly truth is, we three sisters mounted a small resistance. It wasn't Hayley Mills, but it wasn't warm either. We weren't ready for Mike, for anyone. Maybe, by some great grace, you can be allowed a second lover, and in time, maybe he can grow to become as much half of you as the first. But you cannot just order up a second dad, a replacement model; certainly not once you've almost shoved off and grown up.

The first night the lawnmower man—we refused to dignify him with a name—stopped by the house, my sisters and I insisted that Mom go talk to him *outside*, that they have their chat in the cold November night while standing in the garage, on a dusty carpeted stoop next to a small mountain of recyclables.

But no closer.

We weren't ready, literally, to let him in.

I knew what we were doing, and I hated it; I didn't want to be the snobby stepkid you watch on TV, the one who dug a moat around her heart, stocked it with crocodiles.

And especially, I hated playing the part, since Mike had done absolutely nothing to oust Dad. It was just a bad break. And we wanted Mom to feel happy.

But that meant she was dating again, spending more dinners away, and to mince no words, we were scared to lose her, too. Her attention. There were times, at eighteen, when I felt like I had no parent left at all; like a little chick nudged out of the nest, still a bit fluffy, still a bit soft.

So vividly, I remember it; it is one Sunday morning, just before Christmas. The *first* Christmas. Mom has met Mike, and the music is slow, volume low, but it's there: It's coming back into her world.

Our extended family meets at an old lakeside hotel that's famous for their buffet brunch. The place is sweet-smelling, a mix of oranges and omelets, leavened with a faint hint of fish. It oozes romance, the holiday, nostalgia—like a big bucket of Christmas has been tipped over and no one has bothered to clean it up. Glittering strings of white lights and garland vine their way down a staircase; a tree in the corner is covered with tinsel, mercury baubles, memories from simpler times. It is like stepping back fifty years; any minute, Bing Crosby might come around the corner and pummel you with a song about snow.

Our long table—really, several small ones that a busboy had hurriedly pushed together—buzzes with happy laughter and the sharp, salty smells of spinach and feta, bacon, urns of hot, weak coffee. Beyond us, past the row of big windows that make a glass wall at the rear of the restaurant, a white gazebo—one that looks like it is made of iron lace—is iced in twinkle lights. Still thousands more tendril the trees beside it, dimly glowing as Lake Ontario stretches menacing arms wide, her waves cold and seething against a winter-gray sky.

We sit down to laughs and lots of old stories, and I push food around my plate, focus hard on cutting my thick waffle into cubes, drizzling syrup into each divot. I'm not hungry. There is so much warm, willful happy happening here, I think, and no one is even questioning it. It's like a tacit, backdoor agreement that Christmas, this year, like always, can just waltz in. Come right behind Black Friday with her mistletoe, bright velour bows, and peppermint lattes, and the world will glow, sparkle, and snow right on cue.

Like nothing has changed.

Why will no one say it?

My waffle grows cold; I am tired of the one-way conversation running in my head, angry inner commentary, a passive-aggressive taunting and daring for someone, *anyone*, to just ask the obvious, to ask if this is even okay.

If I am okay.

When I can't take any more, I quietly slip out, my gait picking up into a little run, and by the time I am almost out the front entrance, beneath its sprawling green canopy and pillars and blue icicle lights, I am a little embarrassed, but committed, because the only more mortifying thing now would be turning around and walking right back. And that's why I keep moving forward, when I know I shouldn't, storming out of a perfectly picturesque lakeside brunch.

My black heels punch snow that's drifted onto the sidewalk, a small puddle welling in the tip of my shoe and soaking my panty hose wet. And in this moment I want nothing more in the world than for someone to set down their fork and realize I'm gone, to come out here, to stand still and just listen. To let me be vicious and young and honest about how angry I am, how unfair it is that life is somehow finding a rhythm, just steaming ahead; how things like *Mike* are happening.

The trouble is, they can't hear the cries, the sunken ones, the ones whimpering so low down inside. I am proud, and I expect the impossible: That they should just *know*. That they should know to break the glass, that they should be clairvoyant, be able to reach in and pull out my feelings, my heart, so gingerly and gently laying them out, strand by strand, still hot and wet, helping me slowly untangle the hurt. I expect that they can somehow hear me deep, the echoing caverns of an empty heart; that they can see all that hides behind the lip-glossed smile, the easy grin.

I expect them to be God.

I don't know how you move on from here; you don't. *Time* moves. And it moves you, somehow, too.

There are sporadic conversations that winter, in the early evening, in the living room, in front of the woodstove. Lots of talking to Mom while I pick lint off a throw pillow. It is something I am usually good at, throwing things away, tidying up. But I don't know what to do when the remains are so much more precious. I don't know quite how to move myself along fast enough, and I try to put words to this hurt, but it's hard because there are none—I reach down, and nothing's there.

Other times, during these fireside chats, there are a million words—but they won't come together. They stammer and spin out and stop. They don't make sense.

So we just sit, Mom and me.

I brood, and cry, and mostly stare forward at the flames, and when we are done, she hugs me, and we both try to understand.

Slowly, the fire does its work: It warms. It burns hungry and honest and hot, incinerates, wasting the anger down to white ash. Somehow, even if we can't fully say all that needs to be said, the sitting here—the time spent silent, trying—that says it all.

On the night my sisters and I finally resign, we unclench our fists. We give up our last hopes that the lawnmower man fairy tale will fizzle, and we let him in, through the threshold. In, past the garage.

I remember: He steps in. He wipes his winter-wet shoes on the mat and instantly shatters the picture I have so carefully painted. He is not the squirrel you'd expect on the other end of the e-dating site, but a tall, burly man in a red flannel shirt tucked neatly into his pants. A cousin to the guy on the Brawny paper towels—a man's man, Ford-truck tough, with annoyingly perfect square teeth.

His cheeks are red, and he looks down to his feet a lot. But when he lifts the chin, I see his glasses are a little smoky, and a little bit big—so big Rachel will later announce that when he looks at a map, he can actually see people waving. But glasses can't mute the tentative sparkle in his eyes, one that's halfway between a puppy's and the ye olde drawings of Saint Nick. He's tan, nicely roasted, and his fingers are sausage-thick, and strong, and they're shaking a little as he grips a bottle of Riesling in one hand and balances a small armful of single roses, each wrapped in tissue and cellophane, in the other.

The flowers crinkle, and I count them: *three.* One for each of us girls.

Once we let him in, I begin to realize why Mom had a hard time resisting his first e-mail; maybe, a little, I understand her not following through on not being quite ready to start. So often, love is not emotion moving action, but the other way around; once you let someone in—learn to be civil, ask the courteous questions, find that they have mothers and fathers and sisters and brothers, baggage and some broken parts—once you see that they are the living lonely, too, but have brought you flowers, and wine, and breathed a beautiful flush back into your mother, well. The feelings have a way of smuggling in.

And you begin to love someone you didn't plan to, not yet.

Mike tells us, that first night, how my mother has not stopped talking about us; that really, this feels like a formality, because the way she has gushed about us girls, he feels like he knows us already.

That night—or versions of it—becomes more frequent. Mike pulls on various colors of flannel shirts, and different aromas fill the kitchen, depending on what he has brought for the evening's meal.

And the hurt is still there, buried deep, but slowly, gradually, something is taking shape, layer on layer. It's sesame-seed small, but growing. Mike is finding ways to love us, ways we need him to.

Late in May, I am back from spring semester at school and memorizing a restaurant menu like it's a textbook. I am about to be quizzed on all manners of ranch chicken clubs and steak salads, permissible French fry substitutions, and how to sell drinks I've never tasted—vodka and rum, lemonade and grenadine, all tangoed together, with names that sound like tropical storms.

I am scooping ice, running refills; I'm building brownie blast sundaes; I'm asking the cook to "burn me" so my fajita is sizzling and spitting as I set it down and warn, dramatically, to *be careful, it's hot.* I'm setting down huge, heaping platefuls of nacho supremes and wondering if everyone needs another minute to decide on a meal.

It's my first big-girl gig, waiting tables. Running food, refills, miraculously producing straws from my apron pocket at the nearby Ground Round. It's an opportunity I've lucked out with, thanks to the quick kindness of Ann, the red-haired manager who asked me only a few questions before telling me I needed a polo, a pair of black pants, and thick-soled shoes. I remember nodding, smiling, feigning poise, but inside, I was fist-pumping. Waitress-ing is the ultimate catch-22: Everyone wants to hire experience, which means no one's willing to train it. Unless, of course, they are Ann.

Things were finally, for the first time, lining up.

My training near finished, I can't wait to be set free and start trad-ing grins for tips. I am ready, I think, for the electricity of a Friday night, a hot summer full of frothy, free milk shakes, all the Diet Coke I can drink. And it's all possible because, get this: I have a car. Or at least, permission to use the family junker, an ashy blue Lumina that wheezes a little every now and then, but stalls only when it's cold enough to snow. But this is summer, and all systems are go.

Or they are, until Danielle—seventeen and freshly licensed—cracks the car up right before my first shift. She'd been eating a strawberry yogurt, one hand on the wheel, spoon in the other, and then it happened: Mid-bite, she lost control. The car is pro-nounced dead at the corner, just a mile from home like they always say.

She isn't hurt, but I'm stranded.

Not for long, though; without any discussion, the next morn-ing, Mike makes finding me a new-old car his full-time job. He begins scouring swap sheets, circling leads in big Magic Marker, and then places calls to tease out lemons.

Once he's narrowed a list, he drives me out in his truck to see the best specimens—waxed, washed, and parked at that oh-so-seductive angle on the front lawns.

Instantly, my hands itch to sign. Show me the line, the price is right. The interiors are clean, the upholstery vacuumed, the little ashtrays emptied, all the gum scraped out. I crawl inside to fiddle with the knobs of the sound system, the air-conditioning. The vents run cold and my station comes in clear.

But Mike only nods, maintaining a stoicism as he runs his fingers under the ridge of the hood, till it pops; he props it up and begins poking around, appraising the engine.

This happens again and again, with each car we see. I watch the owners; they begin shifting their weight back and forth, foot to foot, holding their breath. No good cleanup job will fool a mechanic. Mike is not into cosmetics.

He pulls a dipstick out to analyze fluid, see whether it's pink or brown, see-through or sooty. Most owners, by now, are slightly unnerved. And they should be. Mike is the kind of man who, when we set up the Christmas tree, sits at the kitchen table, nimbly gluing and re-bending broken ornaments, a card-carrying elf. *Wing reattachment surgery for you, little angel. Carrot rhinoplasty now, for Mr. Frosty.* When Mike had first visited our cottage earlier that spring, he'd fidgeted, unable to relax until we put a Phillips head in his hand.

If the sellers were nervous with the hood-pop, they are downright squirming by the time Mike gets on his back and slides underneath. He bangs round, rough, whacking like a doctor checking reflexes. I smile, sweetly, and pretend this is all very normal, that this is how most people buy old cars.

When he wriggles back out, stands up, and smooths his jeans, he asks for a log of repair history, any receipts from each of the jobs. Then he begins grilling, CIA-style, with "What might need a replacement in the near future?" and "What kind of driving was it typically used for?"

This goes on and on, until finally, we find her: a white '91

Chevy Blazer S-10, with rear-wheel drive. She has lived most of her life as a Florida car, has known only two New York winters. The serpentine belt had been replaced a year earlier.

It is only now, years later, looking back, that I understand what actually happened that afternoon car shopping. Mike had seen the detailed record of tune-ups, and problems, and *that* had convinced him to reach deep into his pocket and produce a handshake and a down payment—one hundred dollars of my teenage money, which I'd handed him on the ride over.

It had bothered me, a little, to see a list of all the ways this car had proven fallible, to know about the rust blistering its under-belly, its potential hang-ups. But for Mike, this seemed to have the opposite effect. Rather than scare him, he liked knowing; he valued the honesty, he trusted the owner, the price. He saw hope in that car, armed me with a pressure gauge, a memo book, and told me to document everything, starting now.

Mom and Mike marry the following year. It is a small, snowy evening reception, held in the same restaurant I stormed out of.

I bring a boy as my date: Blond and blueberry-eyed, he is empirically handsome, with surfer good looks and a deep, hymn-singing voice, and we fall hard in love, as fast as Mom says it can happen. We marry two years later, the moment we finish school, the first minute we can. We are breathless.

And that's how I know.

Over the years, Mike has more than once counseled my husband and me through home repairs; he has made visits to solder our snapped bathtub plumbing; he has helped us chip up a fallen pine after a windstorm; he has coached us, over the phone, on how to snake a plugged drain, how to diagnose the worrisome bubbling that's coming from beneath the hood of the car, how to apply broadleaf killer to a backyard fiercely freckled with clover.

Always, from the start, he has been there with hugs, crinkling flowers, a slow kind of love; he crept up to us, carefully, by serving us. He has given us free rein to be the adults we are, never once asking that we call him a certain name, that we love him, that we knight him as "Dad." And at the same time, though we are not his blood daughters, he drops the "step" that estranges us. He *claims* us. I notice this at a wedding once, when he's flagging a busy barkeep: "When you get a chance, my daughter here needs something to drink."

At another wedding—*mine*—Mike takes my hand and dances with me. He does so duteously, after a black box warning that he was born with two left feet. I don't care, I say. I'm not interested in his feet. I care that he has two strong arms.

And so he rents a tux, and shaves up, and, as advertised, keeps a tight radius, feet planted on the parquet. He is the Tin Man, squeaky and needing some of the oil from back in his shop. But it's okay. We smile and talk soft, swaying, like we're on the sky-deck of the old Sears Tower, and I guess the truth is this: I came to love Mike because he never asked for it. Because he let me do so only after I had spent plenty of time running out of reasons not to, not yet.

If you've read the end of Job's story, you'll notice it wraps up awfully quickly. Awfully simply. Job bows down to the bigness of God, consents to not know, and then prays for his pals. He begs God to forgive them their folly.

And then, imagine, he is restored. Wealthy again. Everything is twice as much as before—double the oxen, camels, donkeys. Double the sheep. That part's at least feasible to me. A bit of a happy note, even: compensatory damages, payment for the pain.

But what bothered me, always, whenever I read it, was the restoration of Job's children. It says that God gave him ten more children, stunning ones. Ten handsome sons and cunning daughters to replace the ten he'd lost.

I bristled here, because it seemed trite. I couldn't swallow this blithe and bouncy hope that God could reinstate brand-new kids; that Job could have the exact number, all over again, and that this would be enough. Really: Was this, in God's eyes, an excusable rearrangement? Did he think you could just swap humans, like you're rotating the tires on your car?

Whenever I'd read it, it'd send me reeling. How could this be the same God who knows how distinctive we are, how unique we are, from our fingerprints to our fears to our fantasies? How could he ever think that a slew of "new kids" could be suitable repayment for Job? That it could ease the pain? It seemed a clean, curt resolution, something better suited to a Disney movie.

This was not a valid solution, I railed.

"God, people are not sheep!"

For a long time, Job's ending would get me a bit angry and hot; . I'd clap my Bible shut, set it down, and it would chip away at my trust. It was a bit of a blemish on God's character, for me; a reason to shrink a little bit back.

One morning, though, I open to the passage again. I have to. It doesn't square with the God I know, the weeping Christ, the Savior who sits with us in the thick of our sorrow, and I know I'm forcing a piece of the puzzle. I have to be.

Maybe I have missed something.

During this closer look, another read, it's like my fingers have found the switch and a light flicks on and my eyes finally start to see. Turns out I haven't been missing something, but worse: I have gone and *invented* something, ideas that were never there in the first place.

See, God never says that Job's restoration is a fair exchange, meant to cancel out all of the suffering. The story never says that God meant to balance the books, replacing all that Job had enjoyed before.

God is fair, God is love, but please: He is not an accountant.

No, that's never said.

It simply says God *blessed* him. That God saw the poverty and pain, Job's aftermath, and conferred new blessings upon him.

That God would rebuild.

And when you begin to realize that Job had come to a point where he expected no riches, no relationships, no restoration at all, but only the promise of God himself—a God who knew the reasons why—you see that the idea of finding new meaning, new purpose, new love in his life was probably the furthest thing from his mind.

And that the blessing probably shook him, the way Mike shook us.

Chapter Eleven

ALL YOU CAN EAT

Painting is something that takes place among the colors, and one has to leave them alone completely, so that they can settle the matter among themselves. Their intercourse: this is the whole of painting.
—Rainer Maria Rilke, in a letter to his wife

One night over winter break, when I am home alone, I slip into the kitchen. I'm going to do something Mom hates: light a candle and crawl under my covers with a book. Mom's keen on candles, just not this way; she's afraid I'll drift off and burn down the house.

But she and Mike have gone out to dinner, so I jimmy open the junk drawer where we keep our lighters, and find two: one out of fluid, one so childproof that, even at twenty-one, I still can't get the thing to spit a flame.

Rummaging around a bit more, I unearth the silver hoop earring I lost last month over Thanksgiving, three rubber bands, and a matchbook from Southern Suppers. I turn it over, carry it upstairs to my room, and scratch the back of the pack. I hold the flame still until it swells and the wick catches, and then sit down on my bed and laugh. Why in the world would we have wanted to remember that restaurant? That night?

It's nothing to fault the place—it was adorable, all gingham and wrought iron, with buffet-style service and full-butter Carolina cooking, and big pillowy biscuits and fried chicken, and, as Mom had stipulated, all the Alaskan snow crab legs you could eat.

It was April, the Wednesday after Easter, and Mom and Dad and the three of us girls had been camping at Myrtle Beach State Park over school break, and we'd planned to go out mid-trip to break up our marathon of hot dogs and shish kebabs. I couldn't wait to put on something that wasn't a swimsuit and eat something that wasn't charbroiled.

By four o'clock we leave the sand, reeking of bubblegum sunscreen and underarm sweat, and head back to the motor home to grab our plastic shower caddies and our bath towels from the clothesline. I slip on a pair of faded flip-flops and follow a trail that cuts through a clump of ferns, the feathers brushing my shins until we emerge at the bathrooms.

I find us three stalls in a row and take the first, hanging my clean clothes on a hook. I twist the knob and test the water; it seems about right, but I let it run a moment, making sure the temperature won't wobble before I start loosening the damp sandy swimsuit that seems to have suckered to my skin.

And that's when I look over my shoulder. My calves are just stupid, cardinal red. I look like a lobster wearing a flesh-colored swimsuit. And when I step under the water, spin, the water sprays and rivers down my back, and it feels like an army of fire ants stinging my legs.

Getting three girls clean with one set of toiletries is almost more sport than shower: I start sudsing with the soap on a rope, Danielle gets the shampoo, and Rachel gets nothing; without Dad to time us, track our allotted five minutes, she is feeling rich and regal and just wants to stand etherized under the spell of soft water. We shuffle the items back and forth between the partitions. When Rachel finally asks for a razor, I toss it to her, and she screams that I nearly sliced her.

Once we've traded and retraded toiletries, we wind up in towel turbans and sprawl over a bay of sinks and mirrors, dabbing our cheeks in foundation that's now two shades too pasty. We try to even out the raccoon marks left by our sunglasses, and paint on glimmer lip gloss, and then hurry back to the RV to wipe on the deodorant we've forgotten.

When we get there, Dad's still in a lawn chair drinking a beer and thumbing through a real-estate guide. He's not sick yet, and he and Mom still have covert plans to move here the moment we've all finished high school.

"You'd better shower," Rachel warns.

And he answers by popping the plastic lid off a tin of cashews. He cups a fistful, tosses the nuts in his mouth.

"I'm quick."

Dad eventually wanders off with his shaving case, and I trade my flip-flops for wedge sandals. Mom asks if her denim jumper dress makes her look fat, twice; we say no, twice, and she sucks in a little and fingers it smooth and then mists her bangs with one more cloud of hair spray.

Half an hour later, everyone's ready.

We girls crawl into a white rental car, in the backseat, sitting hip-to-hip. We're rarely all five squished anywhere in the same car, but that's what vacations do, throw you together. Dad forgets his seat belt and a safety alarm starts dinging, like the car's all annoyed, *tsk-tsking*, and someone dubs it the "Hot Guy Alert," and we titter, loving this new game, looking around. Out Mom's window we spy two skateboarders, pock-faced and growling at the ground. Dad fastens the belt right away so the alarm shuts up, *thank you*, and I ask him to change the radio to Sunshine 96.9, oldies, which I like a little bit on vacation. We're perfume-spritzed and have that happy, hungry feeling, and thankfully, we're not driving far.

Mom starts leafing through her coupon guidebook and rattling off names. We go out maybe as often as a solar eclipse...fine, a lunar eclipse...so this is like Christmas. Wherever we're going, it has to have a seafood buffet, because, Mom says, that is the whole point of visiting the ocean. Dad throws on his blinker, swings into a parking lot, cuts the engine. *Southern Suppers.* I unhitch my belt and start to pop open the door, but Dad holds his hand up in a stop sign, tells me to hang tight while he scopes things out.

We sit patiently, stiff and straight, trying not to touch each other. Standard sunburn etiquette. Rachel's is especially racy: a pale, crisp hand stamped on her chest where she first slapped off some extra lotion and forgot to loop back and scumble it in. It looks like a kindergarten craft, the awful plaster pawprint they make you make for your parents. She has complicated the matter with fashion, too, wearing a hot-pink Hawaiian sundress that vees just a little too far south in the front. Paired with the print, it looks suggestive, just like Mom said.

Dad jogs back to the car and turns the key. It hums, and he puts his arm behind Mom's headrest, cranes to look as he backs up, the belt alarm now chiming again, and we snort: The only men in eyesight are potbellied, with golfer pants hiked up almost to their armpits.

"No seafood buffet?" Danielle pipes. Dad waits for a break in traffic to pull back onto Highway 17.

Rachel twists her head to look out the back window. "The sign says they have one tonight."

Dad doesn't look up in the visor mirror. "I want to keep looking."

Conversation adjourned.

We drive a couple more miles before he reparks, and then wait again. This time he leaves the engine running. Which is good, because when he comes back, we keep driving.

"Let's check out one more."

By the third stop, we've quit playing the hot-guy game. The car grows stuffy and we crack a window. Mom sets the guidebook down in her lap and props her chin up on her palm, staring out her window. I ask Rachel twice to please hold her thighs together, because skin-on-skin gets clammy quick, and I feel the sweat that's already now dampening the bottom of my skirt, and she is amenable, presses them tight for a few moments. I keep my eyes turned low, surveillance, just in case, making sure she doesn't relax them again. I trace my eyes along the ridge in the seat upholstery, a seam that so perfectly works as a land survey, and secretly dare her to cross it.

We go up and down the strip as Dad confirms what he always suspected: Food costs money. Seafood costs much more of it. Dad starts humming along to a Beach Boys ballad and Mom swats the radio off.

We beg to go back to the first place, the country one; the one so close to the campground. Mom says "*Girls*" in a way that curls up at the end. Dad is impervious and keeps going. After the fifth restaurant, and we've been driving almost an hour, Mom quits telling us to be thankful and joins our mutiny. And when Dad looks over and sees the smoke—the steam that's whistling out her ears—he swings the car around and drives all the way back to Southern Suppers.

Not one word.

The car rolls in, Dad parks, and we lumber slowly out and shut the doors hard. We shuffle across the lot in our sandals, unrumpling our dresses and skirts, and when we push open the entrance door and the hostess looks up and shows us her teeth, a saccharine smile to ask how many, Dad grunts: "Five."

We toss our purses on our chairs and mechanically fill our plates. There is shrimp and flounder and pork and chicken. Cobblers and ice cream and sprinkles sprawl, the food chromatic, and endless, and hot. I try to be excited about a slice of coconut cream pie, and Mom plates up crab, but the rental car has baked off our hunger, dried up every last lick of it, and I think we all secretly wish we'd just done hot dogs again.

I don't know who bothered to grab the matchbook on the way out.

Back in the car, the silence is thick. Almost suffocating. Someone says thanks, maybe Rachel, but it is stilted. Danielle and I echo, like mice in refrain. The night is a perfect pitch, tar black now, and we are still dressed up, and it feels too early to go back and choke on smoke around the campfire. Dad must feel the same way, because he doesn't drive straight back to the site.

Instead, he pulls into a souvenir shop. Mom narrows her eyes and asks if we should wait inside while he runs in here, too. He ignores the jab and flags us to come, to follow. We drag ourselves out.

The store is brightly lit, white bleached walls with miles of marlin-blue carpet and cheap metal shelving. There are cockleshell chimes, hung to catch the draft and tickle of a plug-in fan. There's a wall plastered in T-shirts. And in one corner, I find a graveyard of six-inch sharks, dead and bobbing around in glass jars, black-button eyes staring nowhere.

I don't remember exactly how it happens, but somehow we all end up in the same aisle, trying on sunglasses. Aviators, cat-eyed, clubmaster. I pull on a sporty pair that looks like a windshield, and Danielle gives me a thumbs-down. Rachel puts on big bug-eye ones, ones that will eat your nose for lunch, and we shake our heads, *No.* I mean, who wears these? We keep combing, and that's when Dad pokes his head around from the other side of the rack, wearing a pair that's taxicab yellow and so small, they're probably made for a toddler, and he sticks his front teeth over his lower lip like a chipmunk. And we lose it.

"Those are birth-control glasses," Mom says, and we laugh harder.

I buy a satchel that's bedazzled in dime-sized sequins and purple embroidered elephants. Dad finds a tower of saltwater taffy, two-for-one, and tucks a box under each arm. In the parking lot, we ask some stranger to take a photo of us beside a hammerhead sculpture, and on the ride home Rachel's knee rests against mine the whole way and I don't say a word.

Souvenir comes from the old French word *souvenir,* meaning "to remember; to come to mind."

The memories saunter in, sit themselves down, and it doesn't make sense. Why these? Why the bad ones? It's so strange how they just blow right in, uninvited, full color; how I'm getting the vacation back in these bits and bobbles. The candle throws a shaking globe of light against my bedroom ceiling, and I tuck away the matchbook. But the memories don't stop; they keep coming, crashing like waves, running together, breaking into bubble and fizz and foam.

On the drive down we got a flat tire. We knotted our shirts, tied them off with a scrunchie, and laid a brown blanket out on an island of gas station grass to sunbathe while we waited for AAA. Our rescuers finally showed after we'd picnicked right there, Mom making us ham and cheese on whole wheat while we waited, and then we were back on the highway doing sixty for maybe an hour before tragedy struck yet again: this time as a big, yellow swallowtail; the poor butterfly clotheslined on the RV's antenna. We girls spent twenty minutes on ventriloquism, coughing desperate little "*help meeee*" pleas as the thing choked wind, bent around the metal, all three of us whining until Dad finally pulled the rig over and helped the sucker off. She didn't really fly right away so much as she flopped, like a fish doing the frantic dock-dance.

There were marshmallows, hastily charred, and liberal applications of mosquito repellent. Itchy bites. A shoe-rack tucked just beneath the camper door, a rack Mom reminded us to please use again and again. A hot, sandy box of Cheez-Its, and baked brown sugar beans, and red licorice ropes. The way the camper awning got stuck and Dad jimmied around with the broken arm while we propped up the canvas, human support beams. That midafternoon hike to the snack bar, when Rachel's ice-cream cone decapitated, slopped right onto the splintery pier deck, and she moaned, refusing to salvage it, to dust the gray sand off. The Sunday we combed the strip for an Easter service and sat in the sanctuary overhot and overhungry on the hard honey oak pews, praying that the sermon would rattle something loose in all of us. In Dad. How it didn't, and how we left church hungrier and hotter and antsier than we entered. How we drove straight to the nearest Krispy Kreme and waited for the sign outside to blink, *behold*, that the donuts were fryer-hot, and how we bit into them, the sugar pillows melting before we could begin to even chew, sublimating right there on the tip of our tongues. How we polished a whole golden dozen driving back in the car, the box clean but for a bit of crumb and stray glaze by the time we got back to the campsite.

Some people will fight this, but I am firm: I don't think you remember all the good memories. I think you even get a little cheap with them. Maybe you keep one or two of the go-as-planned ones on hand, in the back stockroom, you know, for reference. But I think most of the sunsets and sandcastles and kumbayas get filed away in the cliché cabinet pretty quickly. They're prosaic. They make for yawny stories.

What's left, of course, are your flat tires and your restaurant wars and a whimpering butterfly and a cookies-and-cream cone melting on the boardwalk. They kind of bum around in your brain, hobo memories with no place to go, and in the end, they're more the vacation than anything else.

And maybe that's okay.

The candle shudders, and I rub my eyes. How can one tiny match light such a long fuse? I think about that night at Southern Suppers, eating high peaks of perfect whipped pie that might as well have been made out of cardboard. Mom crabbing, slowly working her pile of crab legs. About the family, cramped so close we were hugging without even lifting our arms. And mostly, I keep thinking about Dad, and what's wonderfully weird is that there's not any anger. Not a drop. I miss him, all of him, tightfisted and clowny and mulish, all his antics, all his flavors melding, all his colors graying. I want the whole man.

I think that's the mercy of this fourth dimension, this most mercurial thing, this one we call *time*. It's one of God's undersung mercies. Time's a river that floats us forward when we can't seem to swim ourselves.

And sure, I admit, maybe time has also shined him up a little. Buffed him to his best gleam. Maybe I'm remembering it all in a softer light, by the diffuse glow of this candle. Or, maybe: Maybe I am just finally learning what it means to love, and really, to love *wholly*: to love in a way that lunges forward, arms out, like God does. Maybe I am getting a peek into that kind of pure ache, the quick beat of the Father-heart that throbs so badly to draw close, to come down, to put things back the way they should have always been in the first place; the Father-heart that so loves, that so groans for someone else so totally that it loves them right here, right now, as they are, even and in spite of everything.

Chapter Twelve

A HIGHWAY

*Praise be to the God and Father of our Lord Jesus Christ, the Father
of compassion and the God of all comfort, who comforts us in all our
troubles, so that we can comfort those in any trouble with the comfort we
ourselves receive from God. For just as we share abundantly in the sufferings of Christ, so also our comfort abounds through Christ.*
—2 Corinthians 1:3–5

The year before I graduate from Grove City, I take a part-time
job in a bookstore.

It's the kind of shop you don't dare bring a toddler into;
the center is a labyrinth of glass shelves, full of scrolly plaques on
wire easels, and angel figurines, one for each month, and miniature sailboats, verses tacked to the hull. By the register, there's a
rotating display of cross pendants and fridge magnets, an arrange-
ment of Easter candles, and, alas, a wide selection of vessels for
Christian caffeination: coffee mugs emblazoned with snippets
from Psalms, maybe a monarch mid-flight.

The walls are lined with books. The youth section, a cove deep
in the rear right corner, stocks slim New Testaments camouflaged

as magazines and gospel bead bracelets, so you can twist truth around your wrist. You'll also find books on purity, inner beauty, boundaries—owner's manuals, almost, for uncovering the enigma of the opposite sex, recently cured of their cooties.

A children's area, toward the left, overflows with stuffed animals; and manger play sets, Noah's arks; pictorial anthologies of the more popular Bible stories; and a row of DVDs starring proselytizing vegetables.

You could get lost in this store.

Sensing this, the shop manager, Shauna—a petite woman, blow-over thin and crisply cardiganed, with espresso eyes that almost bore into you—didn't reprimand me for combing through. She actually *insisted* I do it.

"Yes, get acquainted, learn where everything is," she'd say.

Still, I felt guilty; I worked only two hours a week, on Wednesdays, during the predinner hush when the front door rarely swung open. For weeks, Shauna kindly paid me to fumble with the register, but mostly, to browse while she did the real work, honeybeeing about, never quite stopping, dusting, unboxing, and retagging items, shelf to shelf, like she was pollinating.

But I knew she was right; I had to learn this maze if I was going to lead others through it. How would I be able to point a customer to what they were looking for if I couldn't pilot my way through the piles? If I didn't know exactly where the "walk with God" workout CDs were? If I couldn't point them to sheet music for the Christmas pageant their fifth graders were putting on?

It's ironic that I took a job to work in this store because, if I can be perfectly honest, I get shy about some of this paraphernalia, all the trumpery that comes with belief. It seems an unceremonious reduction, taking intangible and inexplicable mysteries, all the subtleties of this faith, and producing from them so much *product*. Really, scads of it. It sits wrong with me, sometimes. No doubt, there is plenty of substantive stuff here, real protein, real meat—Lewis, Chambers, Chesterton, with words that will wound you, wake your sleeping soul, unsettle you in the worst and best ways—but there's an exhausting assortment of trinkets, too. Spiritual swag. I cringe at the cutesy clichés, shrinking our God to a pencil topper, another flashlight keychain. The black T-shirts with white lowercase lettering: "got jesus?"

I know that Peter, in his first epistle, says we're supposed to cry out for pure, spiritual milk, but somehow I don't think this is quite what he meant.

The longer I worked in the store, the less the tchotchkes bothered me. The problem, I finally decided, was one of *ratios*. See, the baubles made for better birthday gifts. Better first Communion gifts, graduation gifts, Happy Wedding, Happy Baby gifts. And this shrewd little advantage was why they were running rampant, reproducing like rabbits, and paving over the more painful, more precious parts of our faith heritage. And you know how having too much of any one thing, any one ingredient, can change the whole thing, right? Alter its composition? How breathing air too rich with oxygen can even collapse the lungs? That, I think, is what I worry about: that the pretty bits will smother the rest, making it harder to breathe. Making it harder for a watching world to see that we are just as much about the thorns, the blood, and the nails.

I wince because too many of us—me included, me especially—don't balance this business well enough. I happily direct attention to our God when there's not much at risk; a peachy purple smear of sunset, how it's Bob Ross beautiful. *God's brushwork.* A fresh baby that's still ruddy and raisin-skinned, *perfect, a miracle.* And I think—and I think we all can agree—that pasting a Bible verse on a bumper requires a different measure of grit than offering a good, toe-to-toe theo-philosophical explanation of the value of suffering to the atheist who argues the opposite: that such atrocities are proof against God.

Do we bask in faith only when the air is mild and the wind low, the way we might soak up September sunshine? Or do we blush at the first drop of rain, at the first cloud in the sky, and skitter for cover?

This is why I felt so strongly about writing this book; I needed to articulate for myself how God is always present, presiding—not in the sense that he could take part in fads and fashion, but in the sense that he enjoys perfect kingship. Total reign over every wound, every hurt, just the same as every pleasure.

I wanted to know that in the face of something so ugly— death itself—God is also willing to have his way. He is not an analgesic—in this world we'll have many things, many of them uncomfortable. But the world? He promises, eventually, to overcome it. And he promises a staff beside us as we wind through the valley. And somehow, in his sovereignty, imagine: He swears to use even those moments, too.

And why shouldn't he? Isn't it only when plunged into the dark that we can really know our keen craving for light? Isn't this the only way we can find time to forget all the daily dazzle and instead get good and quiet, sit shivah, hang our swollen hearts out to dry?

Doesn't pain ask the hardest questions?

It demands answers; an end to death.

It demands Jesus himself.

As I poke fun at some of what's traded in these stores, let me be clear: These stores are important, and my holding even a polite opinion represents a kind of naïveté. I am no business owner, no entrepreneur. I can't begin to imagine the delicate thrumming of the retail ecosystem, the frantic dance that must go into maintaining it. For all I know, the works of great faith giants—those time-loved classics—might be being sought out less and less. Could their very survival depend on the fine assortment of pencils at the register, the clinking of scriptural coffee mugs?

Still, I worry. I worry we might get lost in these novelties, the way children can get lost in chocolate shops and spoil their suppers.

I worry because, sometimes, the parts that don't taste as sweet really have the most to offer.

It's just another Wednesday afternoon selling gospel goods and music, and by some miracle, I've actually processed a customer's credit card flawlessly; I've tucked her Precious Moments plate into a flap of Bubble Wrap and a box that fits perfectly, and it's almost like I really work here.

It's time to troll shelves.

Shauna, seeing me absorbed in a section on death and dying, comes over, heels soft.

"You know," she offers, nodding to the shelf. "You're new here, but you're already a better authority on all this than I am."

She runs her eyes over the books again, back and forth, a little bit lost in her own shop. "You have a connection with others who grieve, one that I don't."

Somehow, up until this moment, I have never considered it this way—that I might have learned a language. That I am fluent—not native, but passable; that I can hear the bellowing of another soul and carry a conversation that needs no words. That I know what it can be like, in those moments, to shiver, not knowing what to do next, or how to carry on, or if carrying on is even possible.

I look at her, then back to the books, right there in the front of the store, right by the big glass window. And the truth comes full. I see how I've always thought that this thing I was lugging around, this broken heart, was a burden. That I was Sisyphus, sentenced to push my pain uphill, the steep climb, calves screaming, day after day.

But what Shauna sees is different.

She doesn't see the boulder—only its fruit.

I nod, and a fire lights.

"You're right."

In an age of plastic surgery and modern medicine, it's rare that any of us can look at our scars and boldly call them beautiful. But so many old hymns do exactly that; they point to Jesus' wounds, his blood, deeming them *precious*.

Shauna was the first to say it, and I have spent all the years since getting my mind around the idea. I wonder: Someday, might we be able to look at our heartbreaks—our flesh wounds and bruises, all our scabs and little faint marks—and find that they have brought us lessons, schooled us in strengths, muscled our faith in ways we could never have afforded without them? Will we realize that within them we have tasted, deeper, the suffering, the death, the very victory of Jesus? Will we be able to honestly say that the empty tomb is sweeter, somehow, for those of us who still push stones?

What if the grief itself...what if it changes, and becomes an avenue for conversation and connection, even comfort, for others traveling similar roads? What if these trials do so much more than merely refine us...what if one day, we'll turn around and see that they were the red belly we were forged in; that they were the fires that didn't burn us, but *built* us; that they were a kind of kiln we could not have become firm without? What if, in the end, we see: The aches were always as much a part of our story as anything else...perhaps even more so?

These are big thoughts.

I am not the first to have them.

While away at school, I'd acquired a taste for Oswald Chambers's devotional *My Utmost for His Highest.* It's like steel-cut oatmeal for your soul. Combined with the King James English and his don't-beat-around-the-bush style, the words stick to your ribs, keeping you full for hours. If I read a passage in the morning, I'd have the whole day to mull it, weighing his arguments and tussling with the conclusions they might demand of me. If you've never read it, change that soon; do it with wonderful trepidation, because you're in for a ride.

It might change you.

I know, because it changed me. It changed me on a mild fall morning, my senior year, between sips of hot cider, between beads of hot tears.

It is 7:10 on a Monday and the sun is a ball of orange outside my dorm window, just spilling over the horizon, old brick buildings gilded, aglow. I catch a glimpse in the mirror, and there I am, in all my morning glory: limp ponytail, smudged mascara, cheeks all blotch and blush. Last night was unseasonably pleasant for northwestern Pennsylvania, and I'd gone on a moonlit run with my boyfriend and come back so wonderfully winded that I collapsed into bed without a shower.

Now I look the part.

My heart isn't faring much better; it's still a bit tender, raw really, also from last night, thanks to a talk given by a married missionary couple. It was the kind of sermon where the end curves up in a question, asking everyone in the congregation to decide, in a breath, heads down and eyes closed, whether or not you are at least open to being sent as God's hands and feet wherever he wants you to go.

Are you willing for God to put a bit in your mouth? Are you willing to let yourself be *led*?

The call had rung in my ears. Was I willing?

Was my heart pliant, soft, and yielding—was I good clay? Or was I the obstinate kind, a little overworked and overdry, prone to crumble before I would bend?

Was I really so impossible to work with?

I had told God—I had exhaled, in that moment, with little premeditation, head hung and heart open—that yes, I was willing. Or, rather, that I was one rung lower: that I was *willing to be made willing* for whatever it was. That I would try to keep myself lithe, listening, light on my feet.

They say if clay is too stiff to work with, you can take a wood dowel, or the butt of a broom, and pock the mud all full of pits and divots. Aeration. You can fill those tiny wells with water, give it a rest overnight, a good sleep, and then try to wedge it back up.

I ask God to do this with me.

I don't think we ever fully understand the weight of a pledge as bold and reaching as this; when we cut a blank check and press it into God's palm, we can't ever really guess what it might cost. What number he'll write, what he will ask. And not knowing can feel downright vulnerable, bad business; I always feel like a kid parading about in Grandma's old pumps from the dress-up bin, a crunchy old silver purse slung over one shoulder, so long and low the bottom grazes my shins. I always feel too small to be so bold. I feel like a fraud.

But I am learning, that's just how it is; we make promises to God, stepping out onto the waters. It's brazen. We don't know the depth below; we don't know where we end and God begins; we don't know what we are really saying—how can we?—and yet.

We step out.

I think God may be a fan of just-in-time manufacturing. That he would like tankless water heaters and container gardens and instant mashed potatoes. I think he likes the thrill of the last minute, preferring to supply the faith, the fish, the direction, the wine, when the hour is perfectly heavy and ripe. Not a second sooner. He's theatrical like that; he likes to make it so stark and clear where all the power comes from. And so we just have to be willing, open, and bright-eyed, like a child; we have to pull the pen out of our pocket with great alacrity, give it a bold little click as we sign on the line.

Faith is trust. Faith is audacity.

I am willing to be made willing, I whisper, again. It was not the music or the sanctuary's dim orange lighting or the way the missionary man's voice cracked when he gave the call.

I really meant it, God. I still do.

The clock reads 7:14, and I take another sip of cider, slow this time, holding it in my mouth, letting it fill me. It is cloying, so shrill and sharp, and it does the trick: It keeps on waking me up. I shake myself, yawn deliberately, long and low and hard, the kind that squeezes me like a sponge. I try to make my mind alive, alert, ready for what God might have for me this morning. I feel it; he *has* something.

I flip to the day's passage and start to read.

November 1

YE ARE NOT YOUR OWN

Know ye not that . . . ye are not your own?
—1 Corinthians 6:19 KJV

There is no such thing as a private life—"a world within the world"—for a man or a woman who is brought into fellowship with Jesus Christ's sufferings. God breaks up the private life of His saints, and makes it a thoroughfare for the world on the one hand and for Himself on the other . . .

The first thing God does with us is to get us based on rugged Reality until we do not care what becomes of us individually as long as He gets His way for the purpose of His Redemption. Why shouldn't we go through heartbreaks? Through those doorways God is opening up ways of fellowship with His Son. Most of us fall and collapse at the first grip of pain; we sit down on the threshold of God's purpose and die away of self-pity . . . But God will not. He comes with the grip of the pierced hand of His Son, and says—"Enter into fellowship with Me; arise and shine." If through a broken heart God can bring His purposes to pass in the world, then thank Him for breaking your heart.[1]

I set my thumb in the basin of the book, the place where the pages lift and part. And if hearts can nod, mine is; it's nodding hard, and it makes me cry.

I hope this does not seem cheap or fake, because it is absolutely true. That autumn morning, something comes open inside me. It is like this heart of mine has been struck a hundred times by the strong jab of the dowel; like it has been spotted and dotted and rutted and scarred, and then, the water poured over. This morning, it is time: I am set on the table, and I feel the heat of God's hands, strong and insistent and shunting the whole mess of me up and over, until I bend soft, fold into myself, until I feel myself finally coming together.

And my breath catches, and my chin sinks deep down into my neck, and my eyes pinch, and the fight goes out of me.

I tell God the impossible.

Thank you.

That was it. It's like the scene where the storm finally stops. The wind is strangled, still, and the clouds scuttle away, wherever they go, fast, scared as rats. There is sun and silence, and the quiet is so loud, so strong, it almost stings.

That morning, there was nothing; nothing but the soft hum of the mini-fridge in the corner. A hasty footstep in the hall. That morning, I remember the peace, and sinking down into it, and not wanting any of it to stop. It was like a fine dust had settled on my shoulders, a shroud, and I knew if I stood up it would shake off. I would lose this moment as quickly as I'd found it. I didn't want to shut the book, to unpeel my pajamas, to warm the shower; I was there, on holy ground, and I wanted to stay.

I know; I know it sounds so wrong here. So wrong I worry I should leave this part out. But you have to know that at that moment, on that morning, that prayer really came. I mouthed *thanks*. And in that moment, it felt entirely different from how it might sound.

It sounds like I have healed. Like I am a quick girl, have been most efficient in my grief; that I have taken spackle and spatula and just skim-coated the hurt; that, in that moment, I am a blank canvas ready for what God's brush holds next.

But I was not, I am not; I was a broken girl and I am still. But here is what set me free to pray the impossible: I realized that, far more than just being broken, I was a girl who was tired. Bone-tired, thin, gaunt from pushing my stone uphill, day after day. It had been three years, and I was done shouldering my grief like some proud burden, like it was something to lug about. Like it was a thick smog to live under.

Somehow, saying it, this prayer of thanks, doesn't demean my father. Ask me now: I would have him back, no blink about it. *Yes, God, do a Lazarus. Grave, give him back.*

But my heart that November morning knew the truth: What's done is done. I can't just summon him; I can't rewind; I can't rewrite. And so I did the only thing left to do: I decided to lay the burden down.

I said the words, and they tasted a little reckless, a little daring, like I was stepping out of the boat, waves tickling toes. My eyes locked with God's and it felt almost like I was taunting, like I was daring him to do the unthinkable, to really deliver on what he says: to twist beauty from even *this*.

Thank you, Father, for the storm.
Don't let me drown.
Do what you say.
Take this stone and write this story.

That fall morning, the moment with Shauna in the bookstore comes back to me. And it begins to make a small bit of sense. I realize why my heart has felt like a paving project, a jack-hammered stretch of road; why life has felt obnoxiously slow, bumper-to-bumper, lanes reduced, an army of orange cones, so many jams.

I realize Chambers was right.

God was building a highway.

There it was again. Not quite Shauna's actual words, but the heart beating beneath them.

Your heartache is a language, a road, an avenue by which others might meet God.

Chambers nails it; he talks about there coming a point in our grief when we are enough removed from the suffering—not whole, no; not healed, no; but *tired enough*—that we can in good faith seize the scarred hand of Jesus and nod.

The miracle is that when our wounds meet his, when we become brothers and sisters in Christ, in blood, when we come into that quiet, daring minute, and have that nodding prayer, *something happens*: Our hands unclamp, fingers relax. We realize that we are so tired, and we come open. Surrender. We are less precious and prudish about our burden, the grief on our back, and we lay it down. We make it more public, more honest; we become accessible to others, our lives bared before them. We let them come in and finger the broken parts, the scars; we tell these stories, we listen to theirs.

By the community we share, God is manifest. He is there, right in the middle of our love, our mess, our candor, our tears. When we cry, we echo a God who cried, and when we come to the point where we can claim the scars for the fellowship they buy, something beautiful is born. We become a two-way: a bumpy but beautiful road—a rugged, honest one that kicks up dust, even mud, on the dash.

A road by which broken hearts find one another.

Maybe even find God.

Chapter Thirteen

THE LONG WAY HOME

What Adam had, and forfeited for all,
Christ keepeth now, Who cannot fail or fall.
—George Herbert, "The Holdfast"

It's Dad's last few weeks when it happens. When something softens.

We've driven our RV up to our annual summer weekend in the Adirondacks. Dad's sister keeps a place on the Fulton Chain, a string of mountain lakes shooting like a comet right out from Old Forge. The whole family flies in from the corners of the country—Oregon, California, Colorado, Ohio, the Big Apple, more. There is a big green banner draped over the driveway, welcoming us to the Fest, and every five years, new commemorative T-shirts. Pencils. Coffee cozies. We take family seriously, we do reunion swag, we do an annual picture on the back porch, and there is an armchair committee that decides to vote newcomers in or out, mostly based on a thin band around their finger, and we sing a theme song to a flapping flag—maybe because the family is so unfairly gifted, so made of music, but also: Because we are usually *everywhere*. We are an electron cloud of family, always moving—but for one sunny August weekend, we converge.

Here.

We slow. We spend a couple of days calling for loons (looking like loons), reeling in bullheads and sunfish, hiking a bald-top mountain, passing cans of bug spray while strumming guitars, singing around a strong orange fire. The mornings are crisp and damp, but promise fresh cinnamon donuts on the counter, still warm and chewy in a white bag that's translucent in spots from fry oil. Later on, someone tips a canoe upside down and positions it 90 degrees to the far side of the dock, and we all see if we can run clean across it, fast, not slipping, as an aunt chews her lip and worries and wishes we wouldn't, all while she hangs flowered linens across the back porch, a makeshift curtain for a talent show, eight acts long. Some cousins sponsor a pickup baseball game, an uncle heckling from behind as you swing, and there's lasagna—vegetarian for a subset of older cousins I'll never be quite as cool as—and a sheet cake to sum up a birthday trifecta, and we sing, fitting in all the names, laughing at the way they smear together.

When Sunday rolls around, we are tired and full and sad to go.

Getting ready to leave, we are standing on the driveway. Flocking, really, the whole family. Aunts and uncles and cousins. We're slow and senseless as sheep, no one wanting to lead, to move first. To start the hugs. My sweatshirt is cinched tight around my waist, and I've helped load both coolers into the motor home. Mom has unpinned our mostly dry swimsuits from the clothesline, and we've all done a final run through the cottage, checking for Discmans and headphones and stray sunglasses. Books.

Finally, the good-byes begin. They are slow this time, this

year; everyone is so careful to connect with us, and with Dad, to give and gather up his or her portion of hugs. Some people get two, double-dipping by accident. Maybe on purpose.

Dad asks Mom to take the wheel. If you see how long the rig is, and how snaky some of those passes are—if you know Mom's record, crashing into light poles in the empty Wegmans parking lot—you know this is an act of big faith. One of Dad's first great acts of faith. But Mom buckles in, does it gamely even, like she knows she must, and she captains that camper through the mountains while Dad sits in back, all by himself on the narrow taupe couch that lines the RV's driver's side. He keels a little bit forward, his head buried in his hands, palms over the eyes, and he starts rocking. I can't tell if it's the rig swaying him, or if he's rocking himself, but from where I am—lying tummy-down on the bed that's tucked in the back corner of the camper—it looks like he's deep in peace talks.

Like he's rocking in prayer.

I am eight or nine feet away from where he sits. My head's ducked in a journal, but I'm keeping vigil. I'm nervous; the cancer is gnawing at his stomach, and I so want to come up beside him. Put a hand on his back, rub it a little, small figure eights. But the slant of his shoulders is so closed off, so turned in, it's like he's flagging us off. We are all here, mere feet away, and yet, *Stay out.*

Dad's crawled back into his shell.

The rig rocks that way for hours, all of us draped in a thick smoky silence; the air feels heavy on the chest, leaden, like I'm wearing the X-ray cape at the dentist. Like I'm being held in place, walled off, supposedly for my own good.

Hold still.

The Bible says we are God's workmanship, but now I'm

wondering if somewhere along the way I've kind of usurped things. Made Dad *my* project. Gotten too much in the middle. I don't understand the physics of prayer, how it works, but I know I'm supposed to pray anyway. And so I have. I've dinged on God's door, rapping so hard my knuckles start to crimp and crack and bleed, just like God tells me to. And in the end, here we are: I am standing in the gap for Dad, and yet, now I risk being in the way.

Hold still. Don't move.

I am the middle kid, and I am now being told: Don't be.

Get out of the middle. Hold still. Don't move.

Watch.

Because as much as I've tried to be a bridge, a vessel, a conduit, I also know: This business of belief has always, only, ever been between God and Dad.

Watch, God says, because much as I have wanted Dad to want God, God has always wanted Dad himself, even and immeasurably more.

The next morning, it happened like this: I was in the kitchen, bent low to pull a box of Cheerios from a cupboard, and Dad's voice called from the other room. I don't remember what he said, but I do remember exactly how he said it: sweet, tinkling like a little bell. I worried it was because he was weak at that moment, maybe fighting a wave of nausea, but the strange thing was, it stayed that way.

Conversation had become bristly, barbed much of the time he was sick; he was brooding, and moody, and silent. He shot us skipping stones, flat and heavy one-word answers that bounced once, or twice, or three times on surface before they sank clean out of sight. He barked, and snarled, and sometimes even walked away when we called out. The morning of my graduation party, when my sister was wiring up his amp and speakers on the side of the deck, he lashed out, puddling her right down to tears.

But the morning after we've driven home, it's like he's left something in the mountains. Wriggled right out of his old skin. I search his face for a sign, for more clues, and only find more of the same. Calm, like the lake at morning.

Something is different, something has sprouted, but when, and what, and how?

I wonder, sometimes, about that last trip. The rickety ride home. Savoring that Sunday morning good-bye. Those hugs on the blacktop...had they made it all clear?

Was that trip, kissing his brothers and sisters—was that farewell the reason Dad was so intent, suddenly, about nailing down hope? Maybe, with his head in his hands—maybe that was the moment he came to the sharp edge of himself, leaning over, looking down?

Maybe that was the day he and God did banking, shook hands and brokered another reunion?

Someday, I plan to ask.

Not three weeks after we're back from the mountains, we head to St. Mary's. The hospice ward is a sanctuary in the broken heart of the city, and by daylight, the drive there is dismal; plywood-boarded windows, broken glass, chipping paint, coin laundry. Dad is in the passenger seat, sun flooding the car, a ball cap over his unwashed curls. His neck is long and goosey, blanched thin and weak. He looks like a boy.

Mom drives slow. I stare at the back of Dad's head and try to be stoic and quiet and not realize what is happening: that we are driving him away from our home, depositing him on heaven's doorstep. Because that's what it feels like: like we're bringing him to the airport.

A one-way flight.

For all the scrubby edges of this city—with its crumbling concrete, its crabgrass—the hospice floor is a holy place. A warm portal where heaven brushes earth and welcomes tired travelers home. It won't surprise me if someday I learn that the nurses were wingless angels. In just days, they fall in love with my father. He is irresistible now, all downy, all his edges gone. He is bonier than ever, but *soft*, having transformed into Mr. Manners, Mr. Sunshine, Mr. Rogers, cracking one-liners between bags of morphine.

"Don't you all go and vote me off the island," he says with a grin. "Not yet, okay?"

I don't think whoever picked the paper for those maudlin walls ever thought the rooms would hold such laughter.

A Saturday, just a few afternoons before the end, when he and Mom are all alone, we sense something is different. The doe eyes, the sugared words. Dad has cracked open, something's shed, and beneath, there's someone new. We all see it; you can't miss it, because it's like he's sunlit under his skin, but we ache for him to speak it. Enflesh it. Give us words we can grip and hold as hard as we'll need to.

So Mom gathers her courage. She is brave, and bold, and takes a breath. Then asks.

Pat, have you made your peace with God?

No mincing, no dancing, she speaks the question we all have been asking, maybe forever.

And he nods.

He tells her in plain, perfect words, that he has prayed—not sung, but spoken. Not in Latin, but *English*.

He says that he's accepted Christ's work as final.

He calls him *Savior.*

He mumbles a little, running small circles, trying to explain to Mom why he waited, why so long, but they are inchoate answers, like sleep talk; the kind that only unscrew the lids off bigger questions. Mom doesn't press, because it's not the time, and it's not the point.

When Mom calls from the hospital to tell me, later that night—when she replays the conversation, and I have the receiver pushed tight against my ear to catch every last one of the words I have been so ravenous for—my hands sweat moist and my fingers unhinge and I almost drop the phone.

Her words light something within me, like the tail of a firework. I feel the ricochet as it kicks back, hurtling up out of the launcher. There's the shrill slicing of all my sky as it whistles moonward, a ray, a rocket, bleeding coal in its hot hurry. It's a siren, whining and pealing and then—when it has pitched itself up so high it's hung so all the earth can see—it erupts into one fierce flower, a crackling fountain of shimmer and spray, bright and bold and now barely raining.

A big florid finish, before everything fades to black.

Chapter Fourteen

TUCKING IN TIGHT

Everyone must leave something behind when he dies ... It doesn't matter what ... so long as you change something from the way it was before you touched it into something that's like you after you take your hands away.

—Ray Bradbury, *Fahrenheit 451*

I'm back at the cottage, Memorial Day, my seventeenth summer here. Which is poetic, in a way, because I was seventeen the summer Mom tiptoed into the upstairs cottage bedroom and delivered a pinprick that would leak the air out of our family.

I'm on the end of the dock with a glass of peach tea, in a pair of black broiling jeans that suck sun fierce, like a leech, and there's a tiny, tattered olive notebook spread in my lap. It's the journal I take everywhere—to the gym, to church, to a little lunch meet-up. It's mental flypaper, all my thoughts. And as it gapes open, ready for ink, I'm dry.

It appears that, so many moons later, I am still trying to twist my mind around this impossibility: how people can fall away, and yet we still carry them.

It's an idea that has taken some getting used to, this business of shouldering someone who isn't there. It's like a fireman's carry, over the back. Or maybe, it's like a mind trick, this teaching your heart how to lift and cup what your hands cannot.

This is the last secret, the one too wide to wrap my arms around, even though, I'm learning, this is exactly what grief somehow *does*. Grief is a heroic holding on. A kind of onward, forward trudge, making it all the way around. It's circumnavigation. It's sailing up to the teetering and impossible edge and somehow not waterfalling clean off the map. Grief is realizing, by some great grace, that the world really is round after all, and that if you only keep going, one bit at a time, one ocean will bleed into another and you'll somehow, someday, find yourself back home.

I look out onto the water—from a different chair, but the same spot where Dad sat while he sipped one last summer—and the lake glitters like a ball gown. "Why is it green here, but blue there?" asks my niece, far too smart for three, her tiny finger crooked and pointing first to the bank, then to the lake's middle. We take turns, fumbling around with our fake but authoritative adult answers about the confluence of sun, and tree reflections, and depth, and weedy bottom-growth, but honestly: What we should have told her was that this is God's lake and he can paint it however he wants.

My belly is full of deviled eggs and diced tomatoes and ham sandwiches stacked high with hot peppers, and now, the tea. I have dangled a promise (fine, a bribe) to my nephew, one chair over. He's ten, and I've told him that if he can polish off half a Hardy Boys book before supper, there will be ice cream in his future. It's a ploy to carve myself a bit of quiet, but I also know that Frank and Joe are a sort of gateway drug, and I want him to fall hard in love with books. I think falling in love with books is tantamount to falling in love with the world, and having a good appetite.

The book must be working, because he's grown quiet.

I cast a look at the cottage. It's so different now, mostly thanks to the addition of a big covered deck that's been built off the back, like a balcony over the lake. It's a large, lusty thing, jutting out like the bill of a duck, and all ovations are owed to Mike for his contracting prowess, for his sweat labor (which he chased with a nice bit of spinal surgery, over the winter). My husband helped a little—about half of one snowy November weekend—and I sort of did, too, in that I'd sent Tupperware full of tomato bisque to thaw them both out afterward.

The deck has changed the whole feel of the cottage, in a good way. Our family has done what good families do: spider-planted. Each of us girls has married now, and brought forth babies, so the extra square footage is good. And necessary. When we're all here, with two sleeper sofas unfolded in the downstairs living room, our toes all nearly touch.

Having the deck, it's quantum. It has saved the cottage. It's a fine place to sink teeth into a steaming cob of buttered corn as the sun melts the hilly tree line. By night, it's the spot where our husbands play a late-night round of Spades, or Hearts, betting tricks to the glow of a citronella candle, and by day it's a wonderful playpen for the toddler set, sparing them sunburned shoulders and roping them back from the water's edge while still allowing them everything: the slipstream breeze and the yippering of the neighbors' new Lab puppy and the occasional delight of an itinerant ant or daddy longlegs.

The deck railings are pine. From here, sitting lake-level, you can see they're studded with big, brown knots—the kind that ooze an honest, rugged beauty that is nature, that is teeming absolutely everywhere if we'll only open our eyes and look hard and slow to really see. Most people, blessed by instinct and good taste, understand that knots are beautiful. Sure, some might consider them blemishes, pocked imperfections, but these are probably the same sort of people who collect linen closets full of hotel shampoo and never camp, never get any real earth under their fingernails. They ought to have been taught better: *that knots are character.* A run of wood, free of them, looks downright dowdy and affected, even cheap, like a woman wearing too much rouge.

Set down your tea and skate your fingers along the deck rail, into the rim of a knot; trace the whorl of wood, the spot where the fibers twist, confused, and you'll know: Knots are life experience.

Knots are stories, scars.

I read it a while back—about some knots, how they hatch. Maybe it all starts with an arm or branch falling injured or ill, then dying.

And then nature does what she does best: She squares her chest and soldiers on. The tree keeps moving, the trunk swelling larger, eventually swallowing the shriveled shoot. Because...what is there to do, but to keep moving? To keep growing? To keep sailing? To keep making coffee and stirring tomato sauce and combing your hair and taking it all one breath at a time?

And so, a knot is born: a pocket of decaying wood, ring by ring tucked into a tree. It stays there, a secret, maybe until the tree is cut down, or falls down, and the knot gets exposed and the whole lump comes loose, flotsam on the forest floor. Even so: Its imprint remains behind, a fossil, echoing what was once swallowed in wood. Like a handprint, indelibly etched into the soft skin of the tree.

I won't shun facts: Knots can weaken wood. But they can be made to shine, too, real cunning stuff, a bit of artistry in the right carpenter's hand. And so, naturally, here is where I feel compelled to remind you that God is, of course, an arborist, that Jesus spent decades as a craftsman, a builder, working the world with his hands. Of anyone, he must understand the deep truth about knots, these wounds, the way flesh grows into other flesh. How all creation aches to absorb and hold on, how nothing is ever really lost, just tucked and held in tight.

And this makes me wonder if he's wired our hearts to work the same way.

I talk about Dad sometimes, talk about him like he's living, like he's in the next room, a breath away—and in a way, he is. He is, in that his life still has incredible bearing on mine. Maybe I can't call him up or drive on over, but there's a silent pressure he exerts, always, and it's real, another atmosphere, pressing down and pressing in. It shapes the things I do and the woman I'm becoming.

If I ever lean too far into a conversation; if I ever seem overly eager; if any part of me is perhaps too concerned with winning the deep approval of other people; if I perform and absolutely ache for applause, *that*—that is Dad's mark in me. *The entertainer.* Always ears up, attuned and dialed, playing to the crowd. Always wanting so badly to charm, to bend, to give people whatever they want.

People die, but they don't really. They don't. Their souls keep on. If you believe that our bodies house a forever part, if you believe in an eternal meet-up, in the soirée God promises us in the coming grand finale, as I do, then you have to believe in your belly, not just on the soft skin of your lips, that *people don't stop.* I have a pet peeve that other people profess my same big and beautiful hopes, in eternity, in permanence, and maybe they earnestly even mean it, but then when I talk about Dad the same people clamp tight, retreat back into their conch shells. They get fidgety and library quiet and ever so slightly lean back and tilt their heads sideways, six or seven degrees, and cock an eyebrow. They don't look like they believe in forever. They look like they aren't so sure, like they are quite possibly a little bit afraid that I am going to go all Niagara Falls and splash them wet, *Maid of the Mist*, and they'll need a good poncho.

I tell them right away, "It's okay. Really. This is something I do: I talk about my dad, like I talk about my mom, or my husband, or my son. Sometimes I even mention Dad like he's here, and *it's okay*. I know he's gone, but that doesn't take him off the table. His influence doesn't just stop. He *happened*. Somewhere, *he's still happening*. You realize this, yes?"

I sit on the edge of the dock until the sun dips out of view, and the world stays lit for a little bit longer. It's because the sunrays I feel now began their journey here eight minutes ago. It took them *eight whole minutes* to reach me. I read somewhere once that a cheetah running the same stretch, sun-to-me, nonstop at full highway speeds, would take 150-some years.

Two of my lifetimes, running. Just to arrive.

Love is not light-speed or even cheetah-quick; love's slower, surer. No wonder we feel its warmth so long after sunset.

The first trip to the cottage, every year, is like a kind of communion for me. It's a remembering. A moment of holding on, of marking time, reflection. I get quiet, I turn in, I take stock. It's my time to look for Dad in me, and the older I get, the more I see all the wonderful ways he's pressed in, left a nick or a dent or a mark. The older I get, the more I find, the more I laugh. I can know him better, less blurrily, at this distance. I am beginning to think love may be farsighted. I still ache, but it's like the light ache after too far a run, or too hard a go at the gym. You throb in a way that feels like growth, discovery, a way that announces pre-cisely where each of your muscles is. You hurt in a way that feels like you're actually achieving something. You're living and you're loving and things are getting pulled and bruised because they're getting *used*. When that's a heart, it's wonderful.

My baby is in the cottage napping. He'll be three in a couple of weeks, and we've bought him a bike for his birthday. It's an orange-and-gray Disney number that looks like an airplane, with a chintzy little propeller Velcroed on the front. The bike is some-thing Dad would like, I'm sure, because Dad loved to ride, which, of course, also explains my romance with cycling, though I don't get out to do it nearly enough now.

The summer before Dad got sick, we took our longest ride: our thirty-miler, up to Lake Ontario, sleeping bags wound tight as jelly rolls, bungeed to the back of our bikes. In the photo I snapped, you can see my pink gingham pajama pants bursting out the back of my duffel; Dad's got his bag, too, and the tarp, and the blue-and-white dome tent all tied down tight.

We stop after twelve miles for breakfast at a grotty blue pan-cake house where the little plastic creamers have clotted. Dad peels back the lid and it slides out, a big butterball, right into his coffee. We nearly gag. But we stay and eat anyway.

We ride more, talk a little, words fighting the wind. Dad keeps in front and hangs a right into a supermarket plaza, where we buy

a couple of cans of Diet Sprite and a pack of pork hot dogs and gra-
nola bars. And a big bag of Fritos. As I load the bounty onto the
conveyor belt—my bike helmet looped on my wrist, Dad's still
buckled on his head—Dad spins a small toy carousel at the end
of the lane and lifts up a twin-pack of something. Mega Bouncy
Balls. They're fluorescent, big as plums, looking like something
ripped from a solar system diorama. And he tosses them on the
belt.

When we reach the state campground, the sky is silver, soupy,
and it is cool, almost cold, the breeze like a big lick from great
Lake Ontario. But we don't mind; we are giddy and victorious
and warm. What we *do* mind: that our hallowed odometers, for
all their spinning, still insist we are six miles shy of our goal. Our
thirty. But our calves are cramping, so we shove kickstands out on
the pitted gray parking lot, and Dad yells for me to go long. I roll
my eyes but obey, and put concrete between us, and he pulls back
his arm, a real windup, and lobs the first ball.

I don't know for how long, but we fast-fist those two little orbs
back and forth, zinging wildly, frenetically, wonderfully, with no
one else around. We throw, and laugh, and place bets, and shell
out pretend points and make-believe prizes all for catching them;
all for guessing right how many bounces between. Silly, shame-
less, we keep slamming those balls against stone. The harder we
throw, the higher they bounce.

Energy absorbed, transformed, never lost.

We climb back on our bikes and comb the coast clean, back
and forth, until the little computers say we can stop.

The balls shouldn't have surprised me, because if I could pin a
man down in words, shim a whole life into one phrase, one line,

then *that* was Dad. The little bit of magic you never knew you needed.

He was the one who'd stapled colored Christmas lights along the upper edge of the basement ceiling for a late-winter tiki party. It was the year Mom dressed up the brown pole beam with crepe paper and faux palm fronds. They'd already painted the wood paneling a sandy tan and spread an ocean of teal carpet over the concrete floor a year or two earlier, when we'd moved in, so all that was left was to pretend it wasn't February. That it wasn't snowing. To phone up friends, and spear pineapple chunks on skewers, and dig out shorts and sunglasses and the blender. Dad played the Beach Boys—"Kokomo," "Let's Go Surfing Now"— and we even popped a patio umbrella table in the far corner.

Those lights were still up when I got married and moved out.

Another night, when I was much younger—and our cupboards low on dessert, and Mom gone, probably to Bible study—Dad found half a loaf of bread. The bleached white sort that is so sinful it's almost illegal now, and he sliced the crust off, cut it into fours, and painted it gold with a bit of honey. My sisters and I waited at the table, eyes closed, a reverent air as he plated it, set it down before us like a miracle. He told us to open, and behold: *This was manna.*

I still read the Exodus account and think of that night. How fathers set sweetness out for the grumblers.

But there are too many things. Sunflower seeds he sank in the garden that grew till they towered eight feet tall; the gnome campfires he'd always "find" abandoned on the skirt edge of our campsite, excitedly waving us over, our jaws slack at the pancake-sized stone circle, twigs lit with the daintiest, dancing flame.

This is Dad. Dad was magic, had magic, made magic. His

bedtime stories, second to none: I was thirteen before I realized he *hadn't* really rigged a Radio Flyer wagon with an old lawn mower motor and flown to that deserted island, and run out of oil. And had to dig furiously for more in the terrible toothy face of a snarling black dog. Nor had he slept, overnight, in an abandoned hearse; or discovered that old submarine sunk in the side of a river. Dad told whale tales, ones that got down into your marrow, ones that kept growing bigger, and he took such pride in it (and this one *is* true) that, as a young camp counselor, he measured the scare factor of his ghost stories by how many Scout sleeping bags had to be hung out wet on the clothesline the next morning.

Dad *lived*. He *lived*. He had magic, but maybe we all do. Dad just did something with his. He was a tinkerer, adored anything with an engine; he loved it shined up and running, and he loved it coughing, so he could pick it apart and put it back together. Rowboat, paddleboat, pontoon boat; motorcycle, scooter, snow-mobile; RV, mountain bike, dune buggy.

He never got the hang glider, but it was on the list.

There were smaller toys, too, wedged in the back of his closet. That's where he kept the little ones: the bump-and-go Ding-bot robot, with its black, beady eyes and incessant chirping. The gyrosphere, a spinning top that could tightrope on a string bridge between your fingers. And the whirly-bug car. Mike called me last week about that one. "Do you want your dad's old whirly-bug?"

"His what?"

"His *whirly-bug*."

I scratch my head, lost.

Mom gets on the phone. "We're cleaning out the garage," she says. "Do you want Dad's remote-control whirly-bug?"

The toys always arrived Christmas Eve morning, a kind of clockwork. The doorbell would sing, and Dad would always beat us to it. We'd quick-foot it to the entryway, always as he was just closing the door, the sparkly snow-air having rushed in, and he was thrilling, smiling, hands full of a package, a gift that had arrived just for him. We never saw who brought it.

Like so many other stories, it was years before we realized that this, also, wasn't quite the whole truth. The reason we never saw the deliveryman was because he was standing right in front of us: Dad had rung the bell himself, a charade, a little joke. The gift was always a present to the child within; a gift to the boy who was still bouncing around on the inside.

This is what I am learning, thanks to Dad. All these years later, so much of him seared into me, this is what I am finally finding out: We all are in charge of our own magic. We all wake to the same blaring of a too-soon alarm, push our bed-warm feet onto unfriendly cold floors, and shake our Mini-Wheats into the bowl. We lather and shave and part our hair the same way, hunt frantically for matching socks, iron a blouse, fill the travel mug, try not to slosh as we shove the keys into the ignition, and drive to work, unduly angry, real wrath at the slow-sloths in front. E-mail marches ever on, as we thaw chicken and fold laundry—life is laundry—and pay bills. Mulch gardens and mow lawns and clear gutters and bag leaves. There are telemarketers to politely let down.

We can't sit idly by and assume the magic will find us.

We make it.

Dad loved a deal, and the good news is that magic doesn't cost much. If you've got an empty parking lot, tight hamstrings, and the want of a break, you can buy a pair of moon balls for a couple of bucks and pitch your heart out, Nolan Ryan.

If you've got a basement, well, you've got a Bahamian island; and if you've got a doorbell, you can deliver yourself Christmas, and keep a closet full of battery-sucking toys clean till you're forty. If you've got a clothesline, that's a dare to birth a good, wriggling story. And a loaf of bread? You've got a mystery-miracle.

This is why I sometimes take a pint of heavy cream, pour it in my stand mixer, whisk it up real thick with a few pinches of cinnamon or strong espresso until it comes together in big, wooly tufts, and then scoop it, a thick head, onto my coffee. It's why I'll turn up my *Malt Shop Melodies* mix CD and dance in the kitchen, "Big Girls Don't Cry," even though I know that's not entirely true.

It's why I light tea lights at dinner, and last week Googled a step-by-step for folding my dinner napkins into a funny fleur-de-something; it looked like a jester's crown. It's why I took the plunge and dyed my hair fire-truck red, and sometimes, *imagine*, even get chancy with a gallon of paint or a roll of wallpaper, and heavens, dare to put nail holes in clean, virginal walls, because *we get to make our own magic.*

No one else will make it for us.

Before I went to bed at night—before those big stories, before he traced a bit of faith, that small cross on my forehead—I always asked Dad for "an animal."

He'd stand in the doorframe, hands clasped together, like a waiter taking orders.

If I said bear, he'd get down on all fours, lumber and growl and snort all crankily, like he'd been roused from hibernation. He'd arrive at the bed, hungrily sniffing, snout nosing around before planting a kiss.

If I were particularly impish and ordered a rattlesnake, he'd worm as best he could, lisp and slither all the way on his belly.

An elephant, and the hands would swing like a trunk. A monkey, and that manic chimp chatter, the munching on invisible bunches of bananas, the swinging, imaginary vines to the bed.

There were fish, and chickens, and a whole jungle forest full of so many good nights, so much magic, all those evenings, a lifetime of nighttimes, him always tucking me in.

Holding Dad is too big and beautiful a burden. I hug the idea of him, the best of him, the way my toddler shunts a dusty basketball in the driveway, wobble-walking, so peacock proud for the joy of being knighted, being big enough to hoist and hold with those baby-soft marshmallow hands.

This is how I feel, too, arms all full of Dad's legacy.

And it's my turn to spend a lifetime, now, tucking Dad in.

Back into me.

Chapter Fifteen

FORGET THE HARPS

Every day's a holiday here.
—Dad

I know.

I realize that, quite cavalierly, in the beginning, I said that our remembering heaven, its mere existence, wasn't a quick fix for the problem. Believe in it, believe it is good, but wedge it away somewhere. Those were my words, I think, because it wasn't the issue *now*. A heaven teeming with people we love leaves earth feeling awfully impoverished, awfully broken.

And for this, there are no answers.

Even so, I think you need this. I know, because there came a point when I needed it. So I'll take the risk; I'll wager that we have dwelt enough down in the dirt and the hollow, the guttural groaning, the quiet—all the pans of sympathy lasagna, all the lostness, the limp advice. We keep moving our fingers along the silvery swell of our scars, and I hope...I hope that we have spent enough on the empty to earn me a few short beats, a bit on heaven.

But really, on hunger.

In fact, I'll tell you what: I won't even do the talking. I'll let Dad. It's his turn to tell.

It is the morning before he'll be leaving, and my aunt is fetching me from school. Bringing me home in time for good-bye. Mom tells me, later, how it happened; how they are all making peace offerings, how he has made his confession. How they are holding spoonfuls of ice chips up to his chapped lips. How the horseshoe of chairs marks their camp around his bed. They have promised to make him feel surrounded during his send-off, and true to their word, they haven't budged.

There have been moments in this room—the hospice nurses have been telling us that these moments are quite common before someone dies—when Dad's been talking like he's straddling two worlds.

Often, the nurses say, just before people pass, they speak in metaphors—travel talk. As if they are saddling up for a journey. There are fitful moments when their knowing the exact time becomes so absolutely imperative; some of the dying grow down-right twitchy, as if they have an appointment they cannot miss, like some celestial clock is about to strike.

Mom is glancing through a magazine, a cold cup of coffee at her side, when my dad has one of these moments. At first he is silent, motionless, head slunk low in the sea of pillows, deep in his own mind, and then suddenly, he turns, locks his eyes on hers.

"What day is it?"

She looks up. "Tuesday, honey."

He frowns. "Are you sure?"

Mom nods. "Positive."

When the days are few, you fist them, pale-knuckled. You always know the day, the date, the hour.

But for Dad, this is not enough. There are so many Tuesdays. Life, by definition, is *fourteen percent Tuesday*. He moves his head in a gentle shake, dissatisfied. He is trying to put together some puzzle, and the tabs aren't quite fitting; his distress is physical. He won't let it rest. He tries to sit up a little and Mom sets the magazine down, scoots her chair closer. She leans in.

"Pat"—she takes his hand—"tell me why this is important."

He looks away from her, past her. Past the papered walls, past the building's brick shell, past the late-summer sky. By the look on his face, he is squinting, almost—or maybe, he is smiling—like he is seeing something too far away, like he is trying to believe it.

"It's because of Roy," he finally says. Roy is Mom's father; he died just five years earlier, in a bed like this one.

My mom stops still, incredulous, holds her breath, but Dad keeps staring forward, looking into the nothing-something, out and up and away.

When she can stand it no longer, she asks.

"What...does Roy say?"

Dad answers, a slight smile thinning his lips.

"He keeps saying that *every day's* a holiday here."

How do we begin to pet down the goose bumps after hearing this: how Dad talked, one foot planted in heaven, one still here on earth? How do we rub our skin back smooth, tell the hair on our arms to lie down, *at ease*, when everything we've hoped and hungered for is almost tangible, almost happening right here, right now, in this very moment?

How does faith almost melt, dissolve, with this little peek; when the curtain has been lifted, and Dad is telling us that what he's tasting, seeing, smelling, hearing—that what's coming—is so, so *good*?

I think Christians have a poorly painted picture of heaven for this reason: We don't have the right tools to paint it. Trying to describe heaven is like trying to capture the eerie rolling of a sonata, only with a harmonica, or trying to mimic da Vinci with finger paint. Everything comes up short as we stand on tiptoe, breathless, flapping our hands and swatting around for the right words; as if we can somehow pull it all down, make it real, frame its full beauty with these earth eyes.

But language fails us. And that's part of the mystery, isn't it? Wouldn't we have little to anticipate if we could capture the essence of this most perfect place, this paradise, in mere words? What a washout if our final destination, the epitome of all that is pure, a creation singing, shaking—really, rocks shouting, trees clapping—could be crystallized, shrunk, and stuffed into plain *words*!

We can no more talk about heaven than we can reach up after dinner and enjoy a scoop of moon, stir it smooth into our coffee.

We believe this, mostly. Almost wholly, almost unflinchingly. But, in some back corner of our hearts, we waver just a little; we worry it'll disappoint. That maybe all the cartoons aren't caricatures, that maybe we really will spend all eternity plopped Indian-style on a clump of cumulus. That there will be harps and endless dress rehearsals; that we'll be handed a pageant halo, a bit of itchy gold garland to bobby-pin snug in place.

Dad could be happy in that kind of heaven, but not me. I'm missing his music gene—something my sisters remind me of with great regularity. And they're right. I have a hard time manufacturing a chorus of "Happy Birthday" that passes for being in tune. In cartoon heaven, I will need for God to bode merciful yet again and hand me a gold-plated kazoo.

That's why I have to shake myself every so often; I have to reprimand and remind myself that heaven's not droll and vanilla and poky, that it's not some overlong concert. That it can't be all *Little House* reruns and wing-pinning parties, because heaven isn't some hasty sequel. God's imagination isn't suddenly dry, exhausted, blocked. He who neither slumbers nor sleeps is a tireless tastemaker, up all night, and he's got too much an eye for beauty, for whimsy, for art.

Whatever heaven is, it's more.

And that's why, when we talk about it, language breaks. Its knees give in. Words can't contain it. We are children chattering on and on about much too mature things, and the closest we come at them is by angling, by swiping them sideways. We use metaphors and descriptors that just barely brush. We can only hint at the bizarrely beautiful.

That said, Dad's analogy was darn good. He called it a holiday—not by the calendar, but by the heart. I close my eyes, lift my hands, and try it on for size.

Holiday.

In my mind's eye, there she is: I am standing on a shoveled stoop, hands red, chapped cold as I juggle a crock of cocktail meatballs in one arm, knock with the other. There's muffled merriment, the sound of approaching feet, and the door swings open; I am swallowed by a sea of eager, waiting hugs. There's the crackling fire, the candles flirting teasing glows, a magnificent marriage of onions and garlic and butter simmering down on the stove; I can barely molt my coat quick enough. The place is pulsing, always something, someone, more to see.

That's holiday.

Holiday is a world pressed clean, and starched, unsullied. Nothing banal, just beauty. Just banquets. Holiday is the land of forgiveness, jubilee, the realm of rewarding work and sweeter rest, free of bills to pay, diapers to change, milk to fetch on the way home. Holiday is slow; worry is swept up and shaken out the back door. You are told to come hungry, ready to be filled, ready to remember.

That's holiday.

In the sweet heat of heaven, earth and her appetites, all her spin-cycles and revolving doors, start to melt. They drip down, fast, like a sudden spring thaw, until the strivings become a sort of sorry puddle, a false start. What's left behind is small, but it's also all that matters: the people you love laughing a little too loud, leaning in around a table, passing platters, warning that they're heavy and still hot; the world outside the window bathed in hazy, happy light; the fizzy toast of this magic moment, poured out to taste, flutes overflowing, and you almost wish you could bottle it back up; you wish you could make it last forever.

Amazingly, you can. Amazingly, it does.

And why shouldn't it? Every day's a holiday here.

I don't know what they serve at the long table, if all the streets are truly paved in pure gold, or platinum, or if I am all kinds of ignorant for even trying to arrange a sort of picture in my mind. But I do know one thing, right from Dad's mouth—a man who, halfway, had been there.

Dad, in trying to do the math—in trying to fathom what he was heading toward, but could not yet fully hold—he likened it to a holiday. And he balked at our ninny idea: that it was just another Tuesday in August.

It was something much bigger, he knew.

THE BEST KIND OF HUNGRY

They were longing for a better country—a heavenly one.
—Hebrews 11:16

Hear me clearly, please...this is important. I am not happy Dad died, not one bit. But having been there, with it having *happened*, I can look you straight in the eye and say: I am thankful. Do you see how the two are such wildly different things? How you can, in time, learn to be thankful for that for which you are not actually happy? How you can come to count your sufferings as joy, for the sake of their fruit, for all the ways they stir you? That, I now know, was the secret behind my prayer of strange thanks that one November morning; it was a giving-up prayer, a waking-up prayer, a dare for God to begin abatement.

It was a prayer about *fruit*, not the pain that had planted it.

And so, I am thankful in this one way: Losing Dad has roused hungers in me that might have slept forever. It's curried in me a kind of Cinderella dream: a keen ache for something that lasts. Past midnight.

Permanence, perfection, the palace. A world with no splinters, no cancer, no drought.

A world of constancy; a world of bumper crops.

A world without good-byes.

I am not looking through grim-colored glasses; I have not taken up the way of the pessimist, but the truth is, this life is ragged. Scrubby and sometimes even seedy, and we need the liquor of its daily rhythms, all its turnings, orbits, to lull us, numb us into some kind of anesthetized apathy. Life itself is just too much; we can only cast a sidelong glance at suffering, and then must turn instead toward the easier things. To the dog that needs walking, the flash sale on spring sandals, the boiling two quarts of water. We pretend we don't hear the tantrum that's coming from the cart halfway down the aisle; we fake-smile, push past, and walk away. We are polite about pain; we say we'll pray for it. But we do not willingly enter in. We make a living keeping busy, refusing to look close at a world and see it for what it really is: humanity, ripping apart at its seams.

When Dad died, it happened: Somehow, everyone else was losing dads, too. To cancer, to divorce, to the bottle. I no longer could seal off those stories in an airtight compartment; they weren't anomalies, I knew. None of us make it safe to home base. Things always break. Widows and orphans, our fragmented families, are just as true as the Waltons, the Cleavers.

Maybe more.

Dust to dust.

This is the value in death, I now know; it sobers us up, it keeps poking at us, enough to keep us from getting comfortable. Without it, we're the fated frog in slowly warming water; we ignore the mounting heat until we're hardboiled, none the wiser.

Death keeps us on guard. Death keeps us awake.

It would be a lie for me to not tell you that after I step out of the shower, towel dry, I turn to the long mirror, and I begin: I count them, the new spots, peculiar freckles, like my doctor has warned me to. Dad's cancer: It was skin cancer. The risk is heritable. Be a noticer, the doctor says; wear sunscreen and watch for the warnings. Once a year, I make the appointment; I sit on the big chair in a paper-towel gown as he inventories my body like the night sky, looking for new stars. Small, dark stars. I remind him that this is how my father died, and he nods, moves slowly; I hold my breath. I run numbers. I subtract my age from forty-nine, and ask myself if that's enough time to write all the books that are in me, to birth all the twinkles in my husband's eyes, to tour Italy and France.

I don't know where you go from here. I don't know how we get up now and just go brew a pot of coffee, make the bed, fluff a pillow. How can we come through something like this, how can we be so terribly awake and just stumble through the same routines?

I've found myself asking, over and over, what a life sharpened by loss should look like. It should look different, right? We've passed a watershed; shouldn't everything flow toward an opposite shore? There's the groundswell, the shift, the 180, the world changed... but what is this thing that changes in us?

After you've tasted the acrid hollow, how is your appetite not ruined for the confections of this crumbling world? How can you not realize you were meant for something so much more than earth and all her aches?

As time dulls, as time heals, how can we still remain ravenous for heaven? How do we not become once again all wrapped up in

this planet, our positions, possessions, our constant jockeying—
how can we stay fixed and focused on "a better country—a heavenly one" (Heb. 11:16)?

For my mother, it means holding life with a looser grip. Being
spendy, being present, burning your best candles.

It was Christmas Eve, 1996, and my grandmother was sporting a
new crown of pin curls that are common after chemotherapy. It
was better than the wig, she reasoned, even if these kinky ringlets
looked one thousand percent unlike her hair had the sixty-some
years before.

My mom had headed over to Grandma's house a little early,
helping her rearrange presents under the tree, fill the shrimp
bowl, and make sure the electric train whizzing around the Dick-
ens village didn't derail from its plastic track. Both women kept
busy, purposefully cheerful, avoiding the small-big fact that this
holiday was very likely Grandma's last.

There were new tumors. Grandma couldn't see the sense in a
pointless fight. She wanted to live the time she had.

As the last appetizers were unloaded from the oven, and red
and green M&M's shaken out into little glass dishes, my mom
found a lighter and began setting tea lights aglow.

Christmas came alive, the holiday palpable, the way it only can
at a grandmother's house.

Mom came to the last wicks—a row of gorgeous, glittering
pillars tucked into an evergreen centerpiece on the coffee table.
As Mom leaned in to light them, Grandma yelped, practically
dropping a sheet of pigs in a blanket.

"Laurie!" she cried. "Not *those* ones!"

My mom found Grandma's eyes and held them a moment. She'd been so careful all day.

She took the words, now, like an arrow. Nocked and lifted, drew them back tight.

Then let fly.

"Mom, what are you waiting for?"

Mom first told me that story six years later. It was our first Christmas after Dad died, and she was reaching her hand high up over the mantel, racing a match, flagrantly lighting a fancy candle of her own. The taper swirled like a peppermint stick and almost instantly, as soon as it lit, the red and white wax began dribbling down the sides to the base, cooling into a hard, pink pool.

As she watched the colors run together, I watched Mom. She was quiet, her eyes both here and somewhere else, and she seemed at once reverent and daring, nervy even, unafraid and unflinching and free.

To this moment, *that's* why. It's why, whenever Mom or I think the other is being just a little too precious about something, we catch eyes and come right out and say it, like it's the best truth: "Burn your candles." And it centers us. We remember that this earth is only an opening act; that so much more is coming. That there's no point in playing miser, in scrimping, in laying up treasures when God says we should be rich in love, that we should go out and spend it.

So we light our wicks and let them run low, and the flames are butter-bright and hungry-hot; they plumb, pushing deep as they dance and devour; and they glint like the best kinds of gold: They are all at once saffron and salmon and sunset and sand.

I look at Mom, the orange cast on her cheek, and I think: It's a miracle, the way you can manage to walk so far with the littlest pinch of light. How sometimes, even if it's all you have, it's maybe all you need. How if you feed it, protect it, don't let wind quench it—how the still and the small can sometimes be enough.

I look at Mom, and brave my best smile. And we lean in.

Into the light, into the moment, into each other.

ACKNOWLEDGMENTS

I owe my mom the biggest thanks.

She is one of the most intuitive people I know, her spirit soft and good at feeling, like old bones before a rainstorm. It's like she gets memos the rest of us don't. Which is why, back when this book was barely there—a speck, just gaining shape—she was the one who saw it coming and spoke over it with such stubborn faith. She told me she just *knew*.

I've clung so hard to your sureness, Mom. I'm so lucky God keeps on giving me you.

Thanks go out, too, to my husband, Nate. For helping me carve out the time to write (and rewrite . . . and *re*-rewrite) these pages. I don't deserve a hero who's this wise and strong and self-less. You're my best gift, and you make me brave.

I'm also grateful . . .

To Rose, and my sweet, sweet cousin. For understanding. And for being so generous in the places where our stories bleed together.

To Jenny, for so gamely reading some of the earliest pages. For our evening latte talks. You and your art inspire me.

To Mike, for stepping in and stepping up and all the ambrosial meat loaf.

To my two sisters, for walking with me arm-in-arm-in-arm

along this cold, wet road. For letting me tell these things, unadorned and as they happened.

To my agent, Wendy Lawton: I am so lucky that you almost instantly saw the soul of this story. Thank you for working hard to find it the right home.

To Becky Hughes and Adrienne Ingrum and Joey Paul and the FaithWords team: Your belief in this message means everything. Thank you for your encouragements, your good instincts, and for all the right nudges.

NOTES

Chapter Six: Sorting Laundry

1. Stephen King, *On Writing: A Memoir of the Craft* (New York: Scribner, 2000), 103–7. There's a terrific mini-essay titled "What Writing Is" tucked into the middle, where King suggests that telepathy already exists.

Chapter Eight: A Rose for a Thorn

1. Job 2:10, NIV.
2. Job 6:19–21, NLT.
3. Job 30:20, NLT.

Chapter Twelve: A Highway

1. Oswald Chambers, *My Utmost for His Highest* (first published in 1935; excerpt from November 1 entry, "Ye Are Not Your Own" [which can be viewed at http://utmost.org/classic/ye-are-not-your-own-classic]).